Sharon Tyler & Matthew Wunder

Universal Information Corporation Publishing Co.

CRUISE SECRETS EXPOSED

The Insiders How-To/Resource Guide

On Cruising

Publisher's Cataloging in Publication Data

Tyler, Sharon.

Cruise secrets exposed / Sharon Tyler-Wunder & Matthew Wunder.

p. cm.

ISBN 1881999-34-3

1. Ocean travel. 2. Cruise ships.

I. Wunder, Matthew. II. Title.

G550. T94 1994 910. 4'5--dc20 94-76367

Printed and bound in the United States of America

6 5 4 3 2 1

ACKNOWLEDGMENTS

Cruise Secrets Exposed exists because of the expertise and commitment displayed by our Research Editors: Eppie Epstein of Cruiseland, U.S.A.; Bob Falcone of Cruises, Inc. and Nancy Kelly of Kelly Cruises. We gratefully acknowledge the following people for their support, patience and materials:

Jill Biggins - Princess Cruises
Correen Armstrong - Royal Carribean Cruise Line
Doug Duncan - Crystal Cruises
Bill Balfour - Oceanic Cruises
Valerie Gadway - Royal Cruise Line
Oscar Kolb- Travel & Leisure Publications
Paula Meyer - The Big Red Boat
Brad Parker - Premier Cruise Lines
Dan Ward - RY & P / SSC Radison Diamond
Patti Young - Delta Steamboat Company
Tom Boyden - Diana Orban & Associates
Ladatco Tours

Special thanks to: Barbara Wiener of Diana Orban & Associates/Cruise Lines International Association; Scott Koepf, past President of the National Association of Cruise Only Agencies; Thomas Nogradi for expert financial guidance; Renee Rolle-Whatley for her production and publishing know-how; Jill Chapin & Jon Valencia for editing; Mary Ellen Schultz for her encouragement and Mark Weiss and Robin Humphries for legal advice.

Cover photograph provided and owned by Princess Cruises

WARNING - DISCLAIMER

This book is designed to educate, entertain and provide information only on the subject matter covered. It is sold with the understanding that the publisher and the author are not engaged in rendering legal, accounting or other professional services. If legal or other expert assistance is required, the services of a competent professional should be sought.

The authors, editors and Universal Information Corporation shall have neither liability nor responsibility to any person with respect to loss or damage caused, or alleged to be caused, directly or indirectly by the information contained in this book. Although the authors and publisher have made every effort to ensure that the information was correct at the time of going to press, the author and publisher do not assume and hereby disclaim any liability to any party for any loss or damage caused by errors or omissions, or any potential travel disruption due to labor or financial difficulty, whether such errors or omissions result from negligence, accident, or any other cause.

TABLE OF CONTENTS

Cruise Basics

INTRODUCTION TO CRUISE SECRETS EXPOSED

It will take but a few minutes to realize that Cruise Secrets Exposed is blatently "pro" cruise agent. The question is whether this comes at some expense to you the reader and/or the cruise buyer. As you might guess, we think not. Let us explain why.

Our series companion, Airfare Secrets Exposed unravels several little-known strategies for obtaining huge discounts in air travel. Most travel agents would strongly discourage you from reading Airfare Secrets Exposed because it bypasses the agent.

So why does Cruise Secrets Exposed promote using an agent whereas Airfare Secrets Exposed promotes bypassing the common agent? Two reasons! The first is simply because you cannot bypass a cruise agent and book directly with a cruise line. The second reason is that the selection of a cruise has far too many variables in which to make a mistake. An agent is, or should be, highly adept at understanding your needs and fulfilling them.

Pricing an airplane ticket is far easier to do than a cruise because you have fewer variables in which to contend. Price will vary, but there is little difference (or perceived difference) between an economy or business class seat on one airline as compared to another. If you were to compare one airfare to another, after a few phone calls and glances through the Sunday travel section, you would have a strong sense of whether or not your lowest quoted fare was a good deal. Not so with a cruise.

A cruise agent is, or should be, viewed as professional with acquired skills that are vital to your satisfaction. In writing this book, we originally thought of providing the reader with subjective reviews of the ships like many of the other books do. However, we found that there were too many components to the decision that required an expert and which could not be sufficiently described in a page or two. Therefore, we give you an overview of the cruise lines.

Cruise Secrets Exposed will arm you with the tools in which to make a highly educated selection of a cruise and gain the absolute best value for your cruise dollar. Cruise Secrets will also teach you how to empower and guide your cruise agent in suggesting the right ship for you.

Choosing the right cruise ship can be the difference between the vacation of a lifetime and a vacation that SEEMS like a lifetime.

WHY IS CRUISING SO WONDERFUL?

There is a part in most of us that dreams of being waited on hand and foot, playing and sightseeing to a pleasant exhaustion, forgetting about that task we call work and eating while basking in the sun amidst a paradise. Too good to be true?

Megalomania is a misperceived state of wealth and grandeur. Many caring and competent therapists work dilegently with clients' suffering from this delusion. An anecodote to megalomania that is often less expensive and a heckuva lot more fun than therapy is another attitudinal state we have termed Cruisemania. Cruisemania is a realistic state of opulent living in a stress-free environment at an affordable price. Some honest psychotherapists would say that a cruise is the best therapy money can buy!

There are many wonderful reasons for choosing a cruise. Cruises are a great way to visit many destinations without having to keep packing and unpacking and switching hotel rooms. You do not have to worry about inter-region transportation. You move from one point saving valuable time and avoiding the aggravation of bus stops, train stations, airports, taxis, buses, etc. You travel while sleeping, being entertained and dining on your floating resort.

Cruises offer a number of group activities, such as morning walks, afternoon contests and evening dancing. A big plus for many people are the lavish meals - breakfast through midnight dessert. Because meals are served almost around the clock, you never have to worry about going hungry because of missing a meal to sleep in, relax or play. Surprisingly enough, many people lose weight on cruises because of increased activity and the healthy, low fat meals which are yours for the asking.

Many who have not cruised before worry about boredom from being stuck on a ship for so many hours. This is an innaccurate assumption. Many ships have a variety of live music, casinos, shops, boutiques, Broadway theater type shows, movie theaters, stores to shop, libraries and conference rooms plus pools, health spas, basketball courts, ping pong tables, skeet shooting, and beauty salons and jogging tracks. There are guest speakers and videotapes that will give you an overview of the ports you are about to enter.

Cruises also offer the opportunity to be completely waited upon - there are many people there to serve you. Cabin stewards pride themselves in getting to know your typical schedule so that you never catch them while they're making up your cabin or turning down your covers.

Cruisemania is a close cousin to Megalomania. Both center around a lavish and untroubled lifestyle, but Cruisemania is a completely authentic, stress free and highly desired state of being that millions of people have discovered.

Types Of Cruise Ships

There are many modes of traveling via water that vary between the dingy and the aircraft carrier. One can cruise on a conventional cruise ship, masted sailing ship, freighter or ferry. It is important to understand the distinctions between the types of sea-going vessels that carry passengers. Listed below are different types of vessels in which you can cruise.

OLDER (PRE-1980'S) CRUISE SHIP

approximately $100-$300 per person, per day (called a per diem) including airfare.

Economy ships that are generally older and have not kept up with the competition to offer the best and the latest to their clientele. Some cruise consumers think that they have bought a "steal" only to realize that they got what they paid for in an economy ship. Some economy ships are a great value while others are not. A good cruise agent can steer you in the right direction.

MODERN CRUISE SHIP

approximately $150-$400 per person, per day (called a per diem) including airfare.

A modern cruise ship is a floating destination designed for vacations. This is to say that a cruise ship is a mobile island resort that carries 400-2500 passengers. When you hear someone saying, "I just took a cruise," they are typically referring to a cruise on a modern cruise ship. Modern cruise ships offer a vast array of activities and travel to various ports of call.

SPECIALITY OR ADVENTURE SHIPS

approximately $310 -$600 per person, per day
(called a per diem) including airfare.

Speciality cruises are those out-of-the-way or atypical cruises that are either smaller in size and/or off the beaten path. They are chosen on the basis of the destination(s) to be visited. These cruises range from a jaunt down the Yangstze River to high adventure on an Antarctic Expedition and almost every type of journey via water in between. We recommend that you skim through the chapter entitled **Where To Book Your Next Cruise - Speciality Cruises** to see what interests you, then write away for one or more of their brochures.

UPSCALE OR DELUXE SHIPS

approximately $500-$1000 per person, per day (called a per diem) including airfare.

As the name implies, a luxury ship is an elegant cruising experience. Luxury cruise passengers are afforded more spacious staterooms, a higher crew to passenger ratio, a greater likelihood of having a cabin with a private balcony or veranda, formal or casually elegant dining on fine china (typically single serving), impeccable (better) service, complimentary bar drinks and the best of the best.

A luxury cruise ship serves the upper economy, old money, country club clientele that choose to vacation with people who share similar socio-economic backgrounds. While cruising has developed its place with the middle income earners, luxury ships will always cater to the upper income earners.

MEGASHIP

approximately $125-$350 per person, per day (called a per diem) including airfare.

The term "mega" means huge and/or more. A megaship is a monstrous vessel that carries 1,500 or more passengers and is 60,000 tons or more. (One gross registered Ton is equal to 100 cubic feet of enclosed passenger space). Similar to the Modern or Megaship, the Megaliner offers more and bigger of everything: pools, bars, movie theaters, restaurants, etc.. Because of the growing demand for cruise vacations and the profitabilty of these Megaliners, we see a trend towards building this type of cruise ship.

MASTED SAILING OR TALL SHIPS

approximately $100 -$400 per person, per day (called a per diem) including airfare.

The masted sailing ships are an intimate version of the all inclusive vacation which usually carry 30 -180 passengers. Sailing ships do not necessarily keep to an itinery due to the variables of the wind and sea conditions. This can either be a positive or a negative depending on how you view your vacation. If you enjoy flexibility and a "lets see where the wind takes us" attitude, this may be the trip for you.

Tall Ship cruises can vary from the ultra luxurious to the very basic depending on what level of participation you want in operating the ship and how attached you are to the creature comforts (warm showers, private bathrooms...). Many offer sun activities, night entertainment and sumptuous dinners (though the menus are generally more limited than the conventional cruise ship). Tall Ship cruises are typically a more "casual style" cruise, in that they may not have a dress code, except for the Captain's dinner.

FREIGHTERS

approximately $100 -$400 per person, per day.
Price does not include airfare or transfers.

While many cruise lines are in the business of travel and tourism, many shipping lines are in the business of transporting freight but open up a limited number of cabins for passengers.

Cruising via freighter is a much different experience than cruising on a vacation-minded cruise line; some say it is better. A bubbly cruise activities director does not keep you busy around the clock; you are responsible for entertaining yourself. Food is more than ample and generally reflects the tastes of the country of the ships' origin.

Freighter voyages are typically longer than conventional cruises. They range from 7 days to 150 days. Similar to the cruise lines, fares range dramatically from line to line and ship to ship. Overall costs tend to be higher on freighters simply due to the fact that freighter cruises tend to be longer.

Planning Your Cruise

CHOOSING A CRUISE LINE/SHIP

Competent agents earn their commission by performing many immeasurable services, but no part of their work is any more valuable to their customer than matching the proper cruise line and cruise ship to the needs of their client.

There are several books available that give subjective descriptions of the cruise lines and cruise ships. The problem with reading a description of a specific cruise ship or cruise line is that books and magazines are not interactive. While a written description might appear at first to fit your needs, a pointed question on your part might turn what you originally thought to be your ideal ship into a ship that you would not consider given the new information.

A skilled cruise agent will spend ample time exploring your interests and matching you with the right ship. Oftentimes agents have questionnaires and interviews that rival the employment application and interview process. The logic is that cruising is addictive and the agent wants to insure your repeat business.

Not all cruises were created equally. Many ships draw a certain type of clientele that range from the family oriented to the mature traveler. Research your cruise by first learning of the ships "personality". Find out who the typical cruiser is - single, married, children, age, education, interests and what special activities will be on board. Does the ship cater to couples, families, singles, or mature travelers.

Even the seasoned cruiser utilizes the experience of the knowledgeable cruise agent when selecting a new ship. Choosing a cruise line/ship is somewhat analogous to playing the stock market. Unless you are aware of all the factors that comprise making an astute buying decision, you are truly gambling.

HOW MANY PORTS?

More often than not, the novice cruiser assumes that the more ports a ship visits, the better the cruise value. This is not necessarily true. One must first consider their cruise goal. Do you rejuvenate yourself by voraciously consuming all the sights or by maintaining a slow and balanced pace aboard the ship? Visiting many ports and buying shore excursions can be an exhausting and expensive proposition. We are certainly not discouraging shore excursions and visiting several ports, but realize they are not essential for an excellent cruise experience. Many consider a cruise as a destination in itself, and as such, never step foot off the ship during their cruise.

CHOOSING A CABIN/STATEROOM

Take advantage of an old system of cabin pricing. In the days of the older ships, of which there are still many out there, choosing a cabin was analogous to buying real estate. Location was a critical determinant of price and value. However, on newer ships, technology has reduced choosing a cabin to more of a matter of prestige then of comfort.

It is interesting to note the origin of the word "Posh" was derived. "Posh" is actually an acronym for the words Port Outside Starboard Home. In the days before the air conditioner, ships were very hot and stuffy. The upper crust aboard the ship would travel portside out to take advantage of the cool breeze. On the return, these select passengers would switch their cabin to the starboard side for some relief from the heat.

Today, air conditioners have eliminated the need for switching cabins. However, we recommend booking a cabin on the "Port" side so that you may see the shore when the ship is at port. There is no extra charge for a port side cabin and a good cruise agent will alert you to this fact.

One thing to remember is to never trust the deck plan; they can be misleading. Cruise brochures will give you the location of their cabins but will rarely tell you the size of the cabin. The published pictures are accurate in size, but they may not represent the actual size of your cabin. Cruise brochures typically picture their largest cabin on the ship. If you take advantage of the cruise activities and amenities the ship has to offer, you will not be in your cabin all that much. Of course, a person who has experienced a bigger and better suite would vehemently argue this point due to it's added comfort.

THE CABIN RATING SYSTEM

A good rule of thumb is that the longer the cruise (more days at sea), the more important it becomes to select the right cabin.

Cabins are classified into several catagories that are given a rating from A-Q (some North American cruise lines use the alphabetical catagorization system). Keep in mind that each cruise line has their own system for catagorizing the quality ranking of each of their ships cabins. Some cruise lines play with the rankings and use triple A or double C.

There are some universal truths about the "types" of cabins available, however, **how** the cruise line catagorizes their ship can be rather subjective on their part. Most cabins are designed for double occupancy, using two single beds (ask your travel/cruise representative). Some rooms are made for three to four people, this usually entails a bunk-bed over one of the lower beds. Very few rooms are set aside for single occupancy though the newest of ships are more likely to accommodate the solo traveler.

Cabin Rankings

Suites:
Amidship, bedroom and sitting area, picture window(s), bathroom with bathtub and shower, approximately 250 square feet.

Mini Suites:
Deluxe Outside Cabins (generally ranked as A,B and C) veranda, penthouse or mini-suite, 2 twin beds or 1 full/queen size, large sitting area with table or loveseat, good closet, bathroom with bathtub and shower, picture windows, amidship, approximately 200 square feet.

Deluxe Outside:
Amidship or forward, portholes or picture window, bathroom with approximately 140-190 square feet.

Standard Outside:
Large window, 2 twin beds or 1 full/queen size, sitting area with table or loveseat, good closet and bathroom, approx. 130-150 square feet.

Deluxe Inside:
Bathroom with shower, (generally ranked as A,B and C), mini-suite, 2 twin beds or 1 full/queen size, large sitting area with table or loveseat, good closet and bathroom, approximately 130 -150 square feet.

Superior Inside:
(generally ranked as D,E and F), 2 twin beds or convertible twins that make a full size bed (Be sure to ask if they are convertible), large sitting area with table or loveseat, good closet and bathroom, approximately 125-140 square feet.

Budget or Economy:
Porthole, bunk-bed, approximately 100-120 square feet.

YOUR BED

The most common problem having to do with accomodations is when the passenger does not get the bed arrangement they wanted. Most new ships offer twin beds which can be converted into queen sized beds, but not all ships offer this feature and not all cabins on a given ship have convertible twin beds.

NOISE

Once you have decided what type of cabin you want, choosing the location becomes important in terms of noise. Too much noise ranks among the most common complaints, but many noise problems can be anticipated through careful study of the deck plan. Unless you have a certain affinity towards noise, do not book a cabin above or below the galley (kitchen), laundry, disco, facilities or lounges that feature late night music. The deck plan can help you in this regard, but don't be misled by decks that aren't lined up correctly in the brochures. You can accurately interpret deck plans by lining up the symbols for elevators and staircases on each deck. You may sometimes find seemingly well-situated cabins are really underneath a noisy area, while cabins at first glance may appear as if they'll be noisy when in fact they may not be.

Other potentially noisy areas are forward near the anchor and the lowest decks aft (toward the rear) over the propellers. The chamber directly below the smokestack running through the ship to the engine room can be a source of noise to the cabins surrounding it.

Avoid cabins adjacent to elevators; boisterous guests or clattering cables could interrupt sleep. Unless you plan to be an early riser, cabins under promenade decks or jogging decks are not a good choice; late sleepers may be awakened at dawn by pounding feet overhead.

AIR CONDITIONING

When cruise ships were first built, air conditioning had not yet been invented. Inside rooms could get quite stuffy and hot. The natural ventilation of outside rooms was valued, so these rooms were priced much higher than inside rooms. Nowadays, cruise ships are air-conditioned and all rooms maintain a comfortable temperature.

INSIDE VS. OUTSIDE CABIN

An outside room offers a small or large window or porthole for natural sunlight that an inside room does not. If you are not attached to natural sources of light, artificial lighting proves sufficient and less costly. The exception are those people who are claustrophobic. The absence of natural light also has the affect of throwing off a person's internal clock. Some feel that this small source of light does not warrant the extra cost. The benefits of an outside cabin include a view from your room as you sail in and out of port and the opportunity to monitor the weather each morning, a factor in selecting your clothing for the day.

Keep in mind that the windows and the porthole do not open except for a handful of older ships. The newer ships are moving to verandas (sliding doors with a small patio) or big bay windows. You may want to ask your cruise agent if the outside cabin that you have selected actually opens!

STABILIZER

Another technological breakthrough that aided the comfort of cruise passengers has been the invention of the advanced stabilizer. A stabilizer is a fin located below the waterline that minimizes the lateral rocking of the ship. Some are computerized to read the motion of the swells and compensate for the movement of the water. However, the stabilizer does not reduce the pitch (bow to stern movement) so the forward and aft cabins experience more motion during rough seas.

Newer ships have a much shallower draft than older ships. Newer ships were built for cruising in calm water. On these ships, you are going to get a surprisingly smooth ride, wherever your cabin is located. (Generally, the Caribbean is calm enough to not cause heavy rocking of a ship with or without stabilizers.)

ENTERTAINMENT

In days gone by, cruise passengers primarily relied on each other for their entertainment - through talent shows, charades, bingo and the shipboard orchestra. Nowadays, the cruise lines know exactly how to serve the interests of their clients and have elaborate facilities to accomplish this task. Whether you wish to sit on a lounge chair and relax at your own pace or unwind with a blur of activity, boredom on a cruise ship is a non-issue.

Cruise ships put great stock into their cruise director, who arrange activities and competitions almost around the clock. Ships often house movie theaters, video arcades, and computers. Complete work-out facilities including aerobics, weight training with professional trainers, sauna, jacuzzi and massages are not uncommon. Cruisers can play bingo, bet on horse races, skeet shoot, attend fashion shows and beauty seminars, read a good book from the library or do some recreational shopping.

When the cruise package became more a destination unto itself, and not just a mode by which to cross the Atlantic, entertainment became more and more elaborate. What had initially started out as Vaudevilletype acts put on by cruise staff in the 1960's, has evolved into Broadway and Las Vegas-like shows, produced by outside production companies. Competition amongst the mega-liners has created an ever-increasing variety of extravagant entertainment options.

Typically, musical reviews with flash, dance and chorus lines are featured as they can reach a diverse, multilingual audience. Occassionally, a full length musical or one act play will be featured. For a change of pace the popular "Murder Mystery" is sometimes offered and at times passengers are treated to a surprise performance by a well-known star.

Smaller, midsize ships, produce less splashy productions; placing more emphasis on the musician and singer's talent than all the surrounding production.

Many organizations or affinity groups arrange special "THEME" cruises for their members who share similar interests, religious beliefs, sporting passions and hobbies. Theme cruises are arranged by particular groups or organizations or cruise agents arrange special interest cruises ie... golfers, fraternities, "Trekkies," square dancers, cooking, bridge players, etc. on a particular cruise ship. Theme cruises often catch on and become an annual event that becomes linked with a cruise ship or cruise line.

MEALS

Be ready for a banquet of elegantly served food that offers a wide selection and generous portions. However, the belief that cruisers will inevitably gain weight is a misconception. Oftentimes cruisers lose weight on a cruise due to increased activity and/or the healthy selections that the cruise ships cater to for the health-conscious client.

Sit down and/or buffet breakfasts are offered. Sit down lunches are also available in the dining room and a buffet lunch is available on the lido deck with less formal sandwich bars available for those who prefer a simple lunch. Pizza and pasta has become a favorite on many ships. Typically, a late afternoon snack or ice cream bar is offered, in order to curb any hunger which may be mounting before your multi-course dinner meal.

Dinner is served either in a single seating or a double seating. A single seating is one in which everyone eats at one time. A second seating, double seating or two seating dinner is one in which one half of the ship dines in the early evening and the other half enjoys dinner two hours later.

Late night (midnight) snack or dessert bars are offered. There is always a **free** room service. No one need feel that their urge for a glass of milk at any hour of the day will be thwarted.

Cruise lines have kept up with popular, more healthy eating trends. Along with traditional beef and poultry dishes, cruise lines have added many lower calorie and/or vegetarian and seafood meals to their main menu. (Special diet menus are also available.) Many have also adjusted how their meals are prepared, selecting fresh herbs and spices and low calorie, low sodium, low fat and low cholesterol foods.

Passengers who have special dietary needs should request that their agent verify whether the cruise line can accomodate them.

Schedule of Meals

• 6:00 a.m.
Continental Breakfast for
the early riser
• 7:00 a.m. - 8:00a.m.
1st seating for breakfast
• 8:00a.m. - 9:00 a.m.
2nd seating for breakfast
• 8:30am - to 10:30a.m.
Breakfast buffet
• 12:00 p.m. - 2:00 p.m.
Lunch in the dining room
• 12:00p.m. - 2:00p.m.
"Lido Deck" buffet style
food for a lunch alternative
• 4:00p.m. - 5:00p.m.
High Tea - finger sandwiches, cookies and cake
• 7:30p.m. - 9:30p.m.
Single seatings for dinner
• Two seating dinners begin:
6:00p.m.-6:30p.m. - 1st seating
8:00p.m. - 8:30p.m. - 2nd seating
• 11:30p.m. - 1:00 a.m.
Midnite buffet
• 1:30 a.m. - 2:00 a.m.
Twilight Breakfast

Typical schedule of meals that vary
by no more than 1/2 hour

ON-BOARD SERVICES

Important Tip: If you plan on taking advantage of any of the following services that require an advanced appointment, it pays to wait in line to sign up for the service(s) of your choice immediately upon boarding the ship. Oftentimes, services that require appointments are either closed or during inconvenient times just a few hours after embarkation.

CHILD CARE

Know before you go. Some cruise ships have extensive child care facilities and resources (twenty-four hour service) while others are virtually non-existent. Check with personnel who are off duty to see if they might want to babysit during their off hours.

GENERAL STORE/SUNDRIES

Contain your most essential needs such as aspirin, toothpaste, reading materials, suntan lotion, etc....

BEAUTY SHOPS

Open book appointments. Full beauty shop for women including hair, nails, pedicures, herbal wraps, etc... Men may indulge in the like or stick with a haircut and manicure.

HEALTH SPA

Most ships have workout facilities available. Most of the newer ships have some if not all of the following health facilities/services: saunas, steambaths, spas, massages and facials. Many ships include weights, Lifecycles, a variety of workout machines and daily fitness classes.

FILM DEVELOPMENT

Most ships have a quick photo service. This service is provided by either the ships photographer or the ships general store.

CLOTHING

Cruise wear from casual to formal wear. Most clothing stores will rent formal wear.

GIFT SHOPS

Gift shops contain duty free items. Prices can be more or less than at the ports depending on which port you are docked.

LAUNDRY & DRY CLEANING

This service is often available for a fee unless you are cruising on the top-of the line ship where that price is sometimes built in. Some ships have washers, dryers and ironing faciilities to iron your own clothes.

PACKING LIST

Each cruise ship also has a certain style - from casual to formal. Be prepared to dress to the style. If you choose a formal cruise, men should be ready to wear a suit and tuxedo and women are expected to wear gowns. (For convenience, some lines rent formal wear on the ship - check to see if this is an option.) If you don't wish to dress up, make sure to sign up for a casual cruise.

The Dress Code

Casual

men = slacks and sport shirt

women = slacks or skirts

Informal

men = jacket or jacket and tie

woman = dress slacks, pant suit, dress

Formal

men = dark suit or tuxedo

women = cocktail or formal gown

THE CASHLESS SOCIETY

You need not worry about having enough cash to pay for services while on-board your ship. The reason: most every cruise line employs a system called the "Cashless Society" in which passengers pay for poolside drinks, massages, souvenirs, etc... with the mere stroke of the signature. Why the Cashless Society? One reason is that it adds to the stress-free environment that a cruise provides. Though, it can be an opportunity for spending over budget, the Cashless Society is a far greater asset than it is a liability.

The night before disembarking you will receive a "preliminary bill" that shows the charges you have accumulated over the course of your cruise. If your charges are correct, then your bill will be charged on your credit card. If you wish to dispute some or all of your charges, simply take your claim to the purser's office. Not all travelers have a credit card. If you do not, be prepared to make an upfront cash deposit.

The Costs Of Cruising

THE REAL COST OF A CRUISE

Each cruise has it's own fare schedule. The cost of each cabin is easily located through their color coded system. The category number is used to make reservations.

Prices are generally per person based on double occupancy, unless otherwise noted. Single travelers generally pay a surcharge of approximately 150% of the double occupancy rate. Some cruise lines have a "share program" that will match single passengers for a better rate.

PORT TAXES

The cruise ships must pay a hefty port tax to dock their ship in any port. This fee is divided equally and added to the intial cost of the cruise for each passenger.

There are also other taxes to consider. Passengers flying to foreign countrys must pay the applicable airport and departure taxes. The North American Free Trade Agreement (NAFTA) has placed a tax upon cruise passengers as well, $6.50 per person.

SHORE EXCURSIONS

First time cruisers typically assume that the more shore excursions one takes the more they will get out of their cruise. A seasoned cruiser knows that the cruise ship is a destination in itself and that shore excursions can be exhausting, overpriced, overcrowded and sometimes unnecessary. We are certainly not discouraging shore excursions; however, they are not an integral part of a cruise. Seasoned cruisers understand that the old saying "less is more" has never been more appropo when it comes to shore excursions.

A first time cruiser typically underestimates the cost of shore excursions. When choosing a cruise, consider your intent. Is your vacation more about rejuvenation or about sight seeing? A common struggle is determining what the monetary and physical cost might be to go on every shore excursion made available.

Is it cheaper to explore a port on your own or to pay for a guided tour? It depends. Local and ship sponsored tours can be expensive and overcrowded. Many go-getters arrange for a few couples to rent a cab and explore on their own. Others go into the town and city and try to negotiate with the locals for a less expensive tour. There is certainly no right or wrong way; however, please keepthe following in mind. A ship sponsored excursion is responsible for your timely return to the ship. A self-guided or independent tour that is late will cause you a series of headaches. First, the ship will not wait for you. You will be responsible for meeting the cruise ship at the next port. Second, you will have to pay for this misfortune. Walk-in hotel and transportation costs can be exorbitant.

One option is to take a short (1 to 2 hours) city-tour to get a sense of the city. At that point you may want to take a guided tour or explore a particular area of interest on your own. Consider the following when deciding between a guided tour and an independent tour operator or self-guided tour:

•How isolated will your self/independent tour be? Are their alternative transportation options if your tour bus/ boat/helicopter is delayed?

•Will your independent tour expedite seeing museums and other crowded attractions?

•Is the tour provided in English or in a language that you are fluent?

REFUNDS, CANCELLATIONS & INSURANCE

If you think you're familiar with the refund, cancellation and insurance practices of the cruise industry, you may want to rethink your assertion. Many changes occurred in 1994. The research is mixed on whether or not to purchase insurance. However, it is absolutely essential that you know exactly what you are buying if you decide to make this purchase.

There are many ways, intentional or not, to confuse a customer who purchases an insurance policy. Many people buy a policy thinking they have purchased one type of policy when actually they have purchased something very different. Since most consumers never file a claim, it is easy to assume that the policy you purchased would have protected you had the need arisen.

The easiest way to unravel the refund and cancellation policy maze is to provide you with a synopsis of what types of trip protection are available. Then you can thoroughly check the policy you intend to buy, making sure that your particular needs are covered.

CANCELLATION WAIVER

Provided by cruise line for a set fee which is payable at the time of booking your cruise. The Cancellation Waiver allows you to cancel your trip for any reason whatsoever (no questions asked), up to a time set by the cruise line which ranges from a few hours to 72 hours prior to sailing. Once you pass that period of window cancellation, all bets are off. You cannot receive a refund past this point of time with a cancellation waiver. Cancellation Waivers are best used when you can anticipate a possible event that may preclude you from cruising or for people who have a pre-existing medical condition that would prevent them from adequate coverage through an independent insurance company.

TRIP OR CANCELLATION INSURANCE

Provided by an independent third party insurance company not affiliated with the cruise line for typically 5 1/2% - 7% of the gross purchase price. Trip or Cancellation Insurance allows you to cancel your trip anytime **prior** to sailing due to death of an immediate family member or personal health considerations excluding preexisting conditions. While Trip Insurance does not always cover interruptions (an interruption occurs when your trip is terminated once it has begun ie... death in the family, illness etc...), many have this feature built in.

COMPREHENSIVE TRAVEL INSURANCE

Perhaps your best bet. This type of policy covers losses due to delay, cancellation, transportation, medical and baggage.

So when does it make sense to purchase a waiver or insurance? You can only buy a waiver at the time of purchase. A good time to buy insurance is to buy shortly before making final payment. There is no reason to insure a $250 booking downpayment with a policy that costs about the same as your downpayment. Don't pay for insurance during the grace period when cancelling your cruise would result in

only a nominal cancellation fee. It makes more sense to purchase a policy after you have a significant amount invested in your cruise and the cancellation of the cruise would result in the loss of an amount worth insuring.

A typical refund policy by the cruise line is a 50% penalty for 30 days prior to sailing and a 75% penalty 14 days prior to sailing. Some cruise lines offer only a 50% refund 120 days prior to sailing. Cruise line penalties for travelers booked through "group space" are more strict than for individual passengers. Some smaller cruise lines have unusually strict cancellation policies that do not refund the deposit unless insurance was purchased.

TIPPING

This is generally voluntary, yet also customary. Tips are generally paid at the end of the cruise (bar tips are an exception). A 15% gratuity will be added to every bill on mega-ships that offer the "cashless society." This is for drinks in the bars. A few cruise lines/ships have a no-tipping policy which is built into the cost of the cruise.

Tipping varies per ship, but the following is a general guideline based on per person, per day:

Cabin Attendant
$2.50-$4.00
Waiter
$2.50 - $4.00
Asst. Waiter/Busboy
$1.25 - $2.00
Head Waiter
$5.00 -$20.00/week
Maitre'D
$ Depends on Service

CALCULATING THE REAL COST OF A CRUISE

Cruise Package	$______________
Airfare	$______________
Pre & Post Cruise Accommodations	$______________
Tipping	$______________
Drinks	$______________
Port Charges	$______________
Day Tours	$______________
Taxes	$______________
Miscellaneous	$______________
Total	$______________

Now Compare

If you now compare the cost of your cruise to a comparable land package that includes equal services and amenities, you will conclude that a cruise is far more economical than a land package. In fact, a European cruise will cost 40% less than a comparable European land package.

Cruise Discount Strategies

A WORD TO THE WISE

With few exceptions, everyone loves a good deal. This Cruise Discount Strategies section will show you several ways in which to gain good value for your cruise dollar; however, saving money should not be your primary motivation in booking a cruise. Besides, there is very little difference between what one cruise agency can offer over another in terms of price. This is especially true of agencies that belong to the National Association of Cruise Only Agencies (NACOA) who have access to the best rates and special promotions offered to the cruise lines.

The procedure in which one chooses a cruise is almost entirely different from booking an airline ticket. Most of the time, ferreting out a good deal on airfare comes down to the best price available. Most of us are willing take "red eyes" (midnight flights) or sitting near the lavatories all in the name of saving a buck. But remember, a cruise is a destination in itself.

Having the "bottomline price" mentality when choosing a cruise is analogous to calling a travel agent and saying that you are willing to take a flight to any destination as long as you are getting the lowest priced fare - even if you end up in Chernobyl.

Never has the saying,"you get what you pay for," applied to an industry as much as it does to the cruise industry. This section will assist you in gaining **value** for your dollar. Using the "bottomline price" philosophy in booking a cruise can be the difference between the vacation of a lifetime and a vacation that seems like a lifetime.

FINDING THE BEST DEAL

Given the huge variability between the quality, clientele served, size and pricing systems among all the cruise ships, how would you know if a $1200 cruise was the deal of the century or a prelude to purchasing forty acres of Florida swampland? Unfortunately, there is no Cruising "Blue Book".

This is where a good agent becomes so critical (see Selecting A Cruise Agent). One should select their cruise agent much like they would an attorney. Find one who has your best interest in mind and not their fee schedule. Then ask salient questions that give a cursory sense of their knowledge. Assuming that these criteria are met, the next step is to determine whether your agent has a firm grasp of your needs. Then trust the professional that you have hired and let them do their job.

Everyone must look at their own value structure and decide whether jumping to another agent to save $40 after spending so much time educating you is worth it.

A general rule of thumb is to treat the brochure rate as a place to start. It is like paying the sticker price for a new car. Some cars and some ships are "hot" and sell for full sticker or brochure rate, but this is not the rule. There is no universal truth which states that some percentage off of brochure rate is a "good" deal. Brochure rate can be somewhat helpful in comparing cruise ship value to cruise ship value, but this is also highly subjective.

- THE FORMULA - KNOWING A GOOD DEAL WHEN YOU SEE IT

•Choose a region in which you want to cruise (you may not be able afford to cruise this region but this is still a good place to start).

•Compare cruise lines and cruise ships. If your vacation time is inflexible, this will help you narrow your selection. Ask your agent which cruise lines and, specifically, which ships meet your profile (young, active adults over 55, etc...; theme cruises; luxury or "party" ship, etc...). Compare apples to apples and remember that there are several types of apples.

•Find the per diems on all the ships in your deliminated list by dividing the total cruise price by the number of days of the cruise. Then add any airfare. Compare this number against any other number. This number is easier to analyze than the total package.

•The next step is to consider your risk and flexibility tolerance. Look for a window of opportunity.

AIR ADD-ONS & THE AIR-SEA PLAN

The cruise lines realize that many of their customers don't live near the point of embarkation and must fly to the port city in order to cruise. To make the cruise more convenient and attractive, the cruise lines have arranged special bulk rate fares often termed "Air-Sea Plans or Fly Add-Ons." Cruise passengers who require air transportation to the port of embarkation can book an additional "add-on" airfare that is often 50% less than the lowest excursion fare you can obtain booking separately. Since the cruise lines are buying airfare in bulk, they are often able to purchase air tickets at substantial savings, and are then able to pass this savings on to you.

Since airline schedules don't always match up to those of the cruise, you may need to arrive at your port city the night before embarkation. If this occurs, hotel accommodation and transfers would be part of the "**Air-Sea Plan.**

If you don't choose to use the flight portion of the trip, you may still have the option of using the cruise line's designated hotel at the cruise line's rate (again, this rate would generally be less than what you would normally expect to pay, due to "bulk purchase").

If you are flying to your point of embarkation, please keep in mind that federal legislation allows approved airports to assess all passengers a fee when boarding (to go towards federally approved improvement projects) between $3.00 to $12.00. Most cruise lines will let you know if this fee will apply to you, when you book your cruise.

2 FOR 1'S

Some cruise lines/travel agents offer two for one packages whereby you pay for one passenger and the other goes free. Is free really less? The paid portion of the 2 for 1 promotion is based on the brochure rate. The key decision maker is plugging your Air-Sea Allowance into the following formula:

The cruise lines' formula for calculating a 2 for 1 varies among the cruise lines. A typical calculation is as follows:

Original cost of cruise		*$1500*
Subtract out the air	-	*$250*
$1250		
Divide by 2	=	*$625 per person*
add air at higher rate	+	*$450*
Total cost of 2 for 1 cruise		*$1075 per person*

EARLY BIRD OR SUPERSAVER DISCOUNTS

Early Bird/Superfare discounts are pretty straight forward. If you reserve and pay a deposit for your cruise several weeks/months in advance of setting sail, the cruise lines will give you a substantial reduction on your fare. The cruise line will require the balance to be due 60-90 days prior to sailing. Of course, each cruise line has a different interpretation of what "early" means. Early Bird discounts range from 10% - 50% (50% is rare).

Early booking is attractive to cruisers because of the savings. These discounts are uniform among all the agencies and relatively consistent among the cruise lines. Even blocked space is priced at individual space prices.

PRE-PAYMENT DISCOUNTS

Some (a very few) cruise lines are more than happy to reward you for giving them the opportunity to both plan ahead and use your money. Few businesses remunerate their customers for prepayment to the extent of the cruise companies. This is just one more sign of how the cruise lines cater to and compensate their clientele. Generally speaking, prepaying your entire cruise one year in advance could result in an additional 3%-10% savings off your lowest negotiated fare depending on when you pay in full.

Oddly enough, the most expensive cabins and the least expensive cabins are typically the first to be sold. Booking early gives you a better opportunity to select the cabin of your choice.

LAST MINUTE CRUISES

On the previous page we discussed Early Booking discounts and how terrific savings can be obtained. Several publications and common sense would tell you that waiting until the last minute could be a great way to save a significant amount of money. Simply approach the cruise lines a few days before sailing with cash and receive a great deal - WRONG! While this may have been true a few years ago, this is no longer the case.

Many cruise lines now guarantee that their early booking discounts are their lowest fares available. Unsold cabins that potential last minute cruisers perceive to be primed for negotiations are actually offered to travel/cruise agents, administrative personnel and/or potential publicity makers on a stand-by basis at a reduced rate. Some cruise lines allow maintenance personnel to refurbish empty cabins during a voyage. Last minute cruise agencies usually book within **four to six weeks** of departure.

While the trend towards selling last minute cruises has certainly reversed, however, the concept is not dead. Many major national and regional cruise agencies are offered last minute cruise specials by the cruise lines to help fill empty cabins and to avoid going public with this information. The cruise lines typically offer these specials to those agencies with large mailing lists. Clients and potential clients connected with these agencies can access this information through their mailing list, personal phone calls from their cruise consultant or, in some cases, a 24 hour hotline of last minute discounts.

GUARANTEE CABIN OR GUARANTEE BASIS OR "TBA" (TO BE ASSIGNED) BOOKINGS

Some companies will allow you to book on a "To Be Assigned (TBA)" basis for their least expensive cabins. This is also called Guarantee Cabin or Guarantee Basis. If you pay for a lower rated cabin and the lower priced cabins sell out, you may be upgraded to a higher priced cabin. However, do not count on an automatic upgrade.

SHOULDER SEASON TRAVEL

Traveling during the "low or shoulder" season means less passengers and greater motivation for the cruise lines to discount their fares. Low season occurs for a variety of reasons including climatic conditions (slight shifts in heat or cold, hurricane season, etc). Cruising the Caribbean during hurricane "season" does not mean you will be subjected to even a drop of rain. The ships keep close tabs on unstable weather and simply alter their routings accordingly.

Fall
September thru December 15
Spring
April & May generally
considered low season
Alaska
May and September

CRUISE CLUBS

Cruise clubs are usually private associations that supposedly give special promotional incentives to their members; they are also usually bogus marketing ploys. Cruise clubs prey on the notion of exclusivity and the hope of an inside deal. They make their money selling memberships for up to $49 per year. Any large cruise agency and/or discounter will beat a cruise club with little effort.

These "clubs" often offer a monthly newsletter and/or complimentary gifts, cabin upgrades and in some cases, special fares. Often after sailing with a particular cruise line or booking with a particular agency, the cruise customer becomes automatically placed in a database that pumps out newsletters announcing upcoming entertainment, new ships, and special deals which the agency or cruise line considers as a club. Some clubs charge an annual membership fee while others are free.

BECOME A TOUR CONDUCTOR AKA GROUP ORGANIZER

The cruise lines simply say that anyone who can reel in approximately 10-15 or more people is considered a tour conductor "TC" or a "Group Organizer." No qualifications, experience or responsibilities (unless your group blames you for any mishaps) are required. So why would anyone choose to be considered a TC or Group Organizer? A TC cruises for free - sort of!

Many of us belong to an organization or club in which gathering 10-15 people might be an easy task. Keep in mind that cruise lines do not require a group to have some sort of affiliation and that 10-15 passengers is a generally accepted number; but this number may vary from cruise line to cruise line.

The question is, "Is free really FREE". The answer is NO, for several reasons:

- Air transportation may not be included.
- Port charges are not included.
- Shore excursions are not free.
- Tipping is not included.
- Spending money is not included.
- Not all cabin categories qualify towards earning a "TC".

The cruise line designates the catagory and it is usually not their least expensive cabin.

Another big question remains. "Is it better to have one person receive a 'free' cruise or can the entire group be rewarded with the cost for one person subtracted from the total cruise bill?"

REPOSITIONING CRUISES

Just as the whales migrate south for the winter and head north for the summer, cruise lines seasonally reposition their ships to areas that are climatically favorable.

When the cruise ships set sail on this long journey, they offer great discounts to cruise bargain hunters. Each time a cruise ship leaves the dock with any empty cabin, they have lost revenue forever. So Cruise lines offer terrific deals to attract passengers on this journey. Cruise companies even offer arrangements whereby the passenger only cruises for a segment of the trek.

Typically, the best time to take advantage of repositioning cruises are in the Fall (September & October) and in Spring (April & May). You may be able to secure additional discounts on a repositioning cruise if you have sailed with the cruise line previously. Lastly, some cruise lines offer an extra large early booking discount on repositioning cruises.

WORKING FOR A CRUISE LINE

Permanent Positions

As more people take cruises and more ships are built to accomodate this increased business, more and more people will be needed to work on cruise ships. Permanent and temporary positions aboard ships can be a fabulous way of floating through paradise. Having said all this, there are not a plethora of job positions available for Americans unless they are seeking specialized positions.

Guest Lecturers

Teaching a class or being a guest lecturer aboard a ship can be an opportunity to cruise for free with limited responsibilities. Classes are taught throughout the day on a variety of topics that range from the culturally enlightening to the art of shopping. Of course, it is your responsibility to sell the cruise line on your particular area of expertise. If obtaining a position with a cruise line is of more interest to you, we recommend reading a book entitled, *How To Get a Job With A Cruise Line* by Mary Fallon Miller.

How To Book Your Cruise

CAVEAT EMPTOR
LET THE BUYER BEWARE

Cruising is one of the fastest growing businesses in the world. Of course, when any industry proves itself to be profitable, it usually entices an equal apportionment of quick-buck artists. The cruise industry is no exception.

Similar to many job positions, there is a huge disparity between a cruise agent and a "great" cruise agent. To complicate matters, there is no regulatory body within the industry to enforce even a minimal level of standards. However, there are two organizations you should be aware of: CLIA and NACOA which are explained after Choosing An Agent - Questions & Tips. We highly recommend that you seek out a competent, service minded agency that wants to invest in your long term business.

SELECTING AN AGENT

The following is a checklist/ interview questionnaire which we recommend using when seeking out a cruise/travel agent.

❑ How long has the agency been in business? Do they have references of satisfied cruisers? Will the agent spend a "reasonable" amount of time answering your important questions or do they strike you as an order fulfillment house?

❑ Does the agency actually have a store or office for you to come and speak with their agents or is run out of their home? Some large national agencies will have local cruise consultants who work out of their homes. In these cases, the main office is responsible for billing, processing and ticketing. The local agent is a consultant only.

❑ Is the agent/agency willing to send you brochures before booking your cruise? If they request that you go into your local agency to pick up cruise line brochures, this indicates a lack of stability and cheapness, an inadequate baseline level of service and should be a bright red flag. (Yes, this does happen!)

❑ Because a cruise agent must match your personality with the personality of the ship, choose an agent who has been to the destination you are interested in and/or has been on the ship they are recommending.

❑ Avoid agencies that ask you to shop for the lowest price and then come to them. Would you use the same tactic when choosing a doctor or attorney?

❑ Be aware of the old Bait and Switch. Some unscrupulous agencies will advertise an outstanding bargain on a particular ship(s). When you call to inquire or book, they tell you that this particular cruise is sold out, but that they do have either a more expensive cruise available or a different ship available at the same cost.

❑ Use a credit card. Make sure that the credit card is processed by the cruise line and not the cruise agency. Credit cards protect and stand behind their customers when a dispute arises. If you pay by check or cash, ask your agent if your partial or full payment towards your cruise will be placed in a "special" or "trust" account. Ask the agent for the bank and account number. Be wary of agencies that place funds into their general account.

❑ Have a considerable number of complaints been lodged against the agency through the Better Business Bureau?

❑ Perhaps the most important tip we can offer is to remind you to trust your instincts. If a little voice tells you that something is not quite right with your cruise agent or agency, try to gain further clarity or simply walk away.

THE ALL CRUISE AGENCY VS. A FULL SERVICE AGENCY

An all cruise agency sells nothing but cruises. A full service travel agency sells airline tickets, train tickets, accommodations, etc. So which type of agency should you purchase your cruise ticket from? It depends on who you ask.

As in any business, when a vendor sells a lot of its supplier's product, the supplier looks first to their top producing vendors to offer incentive deals to unload an excess quantity of the supplier's product. Such is the case with the relationship between the cruise company and the travel agency.

The name of the game is volume. The agency that sells the most of that cruise line's product will probably have more group dates and lower rates. So when you shop an agency, make sure the agency sells a lot of cruises. But remember, price is not everything. Getting a good fare on the S.S. Minnow could cost you more than paying a little extra with an agent who will book the right ship for you.

Because cruising is the fastest growing segment of the travel industry and we now live in a world of specialization, the all-cruise agency emerged to do only one thing; sell cruises. The logic is that if the all-cruise agency devotes all of their time selling cruises, they will become an expert in their field and therefore sell more cruises.

When an agency sells a lot of cruises, the cruise lines may be able to offer a more favorable rate to these high producers. In turn, this agency is *able* to pass this savings on to their customer.

The full service travel agency counters this selling strategy with the point that travelers can expect a higher level of service because they can handle all of your vacation, not just the cruise portion. Keep in mind that an all-cruise agency can offer pre and post cruise tours, hotels and airfare. Full service travel agents also claim that many of their agents are also experienced cruisers who know the ships as well, if not better, than many cruise agents.

When it comes down to booking your cruise vacation, deciding between a Full-Service Agency and a Cruise Travel Agency should be predicated on which agent/agency has the most experience and service regardless of whether or not they specialize exclusively in cruises. As a general rule however, full service travel agencies do not sell as many cruises as do Cruise Only Agencies. Also note that national cruise agencies may have access to bigger discounts because of their volume. All cruise agencies also have land options, hotels and tours that are sold as part of the cruise package and sold by a cruise only agent.

Choose an agent who is best able to advise you on your important questions: destinations, cruise lines, specific ships, and value for your cruise dollar. What level of service do you expect? The quality of service ranges from the two minute phone order fulfillment to an in-depth cruise needs assessment, complimentary bon voyage champagne when you embark and a follow-up phone call after your cruise to discuss your trip.

WILL I SAVE MONEY IF I BOOK WITHOUT AN AGENT

NO! We recommend that you use some sort of travel agent and/or cruise agent. Why? First of all, most cruise lines do not sell directly to the public. But most importantly, cruise agents or travel agents should **not** be viewed as middle men who tack on an extra profit. Cruise agents or travel agents are best described as distributors vital to the dissemination of the cruise lines product whose commission is paid directly by the cruise line.

Only the travel agency or cruise agency is able to obtain any discounts and they are able to accomplish this due to high volume with a particular cruise line. Some cruise lines, especially the top end lines, have a strict no discount policy to anyone or any agency.

CLIA
CRUISE LINE INTERNATIONAL ASSOCIATION

Created in 1975, this organization represents 98% of the cruise capacity marketed in North America. The function of CLIA is to promote common cruising standards within its membership. CLIA's main objective is to raise awareness about the cruise experience. In doing so, CLIA functions as a cruise specific public relations firm that promotes public awareness and holds members (cruise lines) responsible for maintaining high and uniform standards. This organization directly impacts the quality of the cruise experience that the consumer enjoys. CLIA also provides agent certification in its Master Cruise Counselor Certification program; a respected educational program.

NACOA
NATIONAL ASSOCIATION OF CRUISE ONLY AGENCIES

NACOA is the only trade association dedicated solely to the cruise vacation product and the cruise professionals who sell it. NACOA insures a high standard among its membership. NACOA's programs include sales training, educational programs, ship inspections, conferences, Errors and Omissions Insurance, SafeSail Insurance and networking among the best cruise professionals and cruise professionals in the industry. NACOA informs its members of the trends and legislative issues that effect the industry. NACOA also provides accredited educational courses for CLIA's Master Cruise Counselor Certification and arranges agent ship inspections.

Cruise Line And Cruise Ship Directory

AMERICAN HAWAII CRUISES

Kearney SL
San Francisco, CA 94108

Ships: Independence, Constitution.
Destinations: Year-round cruises of Hawaiian Islands.
Description: Youth recreation center. Singles rate and themed cruises. At American Hawaii Cruises a relaxed atmosphere is created by their American crew, and with only one day spent at sea, passengers have plenty of time to spend ashore. Departing from Honolulu, American Hawaii's two ships sail for 2, 4, and 7 days, stopping at Maui, Kauai, and Kona and Hilo on the Big Island.

American Hawaii Cruises, headquartered in San Francisco, CA, the only cruise line operating in the Hawaiian Islands, offers seven-day cruises on sister ships *Independence* and *Constitution* (built in the United States in 1951). Leaving Honolulu every Saturday, the 30,090-gross register-ton/778-passenger vessels visit: Nawiliwili, Kauai; Kona and Hilo, Hawaii; and Kahului, Maui. As the only American-flag ocean-going ships in service, they are the only ones allowed to make such inter-island port calls.

Sailing the islands since 1980, the highly successful ships are characterized as "Hawaii's Floating Islands," and full-scale activities onboard coordinate well with the seemingly endless shore excursions (more than 50) that range from a helicopter trip over the Na Pali Coast to biking down from the 10,000-foot-high summit of Mt. Haleakala. And, what would a visit to Hawaii be without the traditional luau?

American Hawaii has created a most attractive selection of resorts, hotels, and condominiums that can be enjoyed in conjunction with any of the cruises. These are available on: Maui, "The Valley Island"; Kauai, "The Garden Island-'; Hawaii, "The Big Island"; or on Oahu. Three and four-day cruises can be combined with four and three-day island stays for a complete cruise/resort vacation. Most passengers spend two nights in Honolulu (usually at Waikiki) pre or post-cruise.

Everything about the cruises aboard the *Independence* and the *Constitution* is American/Polynesian casual. It is service with a smile at all times. Cabins are large by today's standards, and there are 14 categories ranging from an Owner's Suite on each ship to Budget Inside Cabins.

More than $25 million has been spent on the two ships during the past few years in a long-range modernization program. Public rooms are commodious, and two swimming pools are centers of activities on the huge sun decks. Each ship has two dining rooms where the cuisine features American and Polynesian dishes, fresh fruits, and tasty desserts. There are special theme nights in the dining rooms.

American Hawaii has a number of "theme" cruises from "Save the Whale" in March to "Aloha Week Celebration" in September. Onboard programs offer coordinating lectures in conjunction with the theme cruises. There is a special package for honeymooners, and the line has offered a "Free Kids" program during summer months and has trained counselors onboard who work with the youngsters.

CARNIVAL CRUISE LINES

N.W. 87th Av.
Miami, FL, 33178-2428

Ships: Tropicale, Jubilee, Celebration, Festivale, Holiday, Sensation, Fantasy, Ecstasy, Sensation and Imagination.
Destinations: Caribbean, Mexican Riviera, Panama Canal.
Description: Toddlers' program, health and fitness program, spa menu." Cruise the Most Popular Cruise line in the World." Carnival's "Fun Ships" are the best vacation value for any age. New for '93 - six special sailings into the Panama Canal. The Bahamas: 3 & 4 days; 5, 6, 7 day cruises & Orlando vacations. The Caribbean: 7 days. The Mexican Riviera: 7 days. The Panama Canal: 10 & 11 days.

CARNIVAL CRUISE LINES, one of the most financially successful and popular cruise lines, is based in Miami, FL. With nine ships, including several "SuperLiners," Carnival is also the largest cruise line in the world in terms of passenger loads with one-fourth of the total North American market.

The line started relatively late in 1972 with one ship, the aging 1,150-passenger *Mardi Gras.* After a rocky start and almost three years of losses, Carnival's "Fun Ship" concept began to catch on as a total recreation vacation filled with shipboard activities rather than just a relaxing way to get from port to port.

Carnival added the 1,250-passenger *Carnivale* in 1975 and the 1,400-passenger *Festivale* in 1977—considered huge at the time at 38,000 gross register tons. When the company announced in 1978 it would build a new ship, the industry was stunned. Ship construction and fuel costs were at an all-time high. The result, however, was the 1,400-passenger *Tropicale* in 1982, a catalyst for more than $1 billion in new ship construction industry-wide over the next decade.

Carnival has rarely ventured outside the warm waters of the Caribbean and Mexico. Its super liners of the 1980s—the 1,800 passenger *Holiday* ('85), 1,896-passenger *Jubilee* ('86), and 1,896-passenger *Celebration* ('87)—all sail out of Miami or Los Angeles on seven-night cruises.

With the advent of the giant 2,600-passenger Fantasy into the three and four day cruise market to the Bahamas from Miami, Carnival relegated the oldest ships, *Mardi Gras* and *Carnivale,* to similar short cruises to the Bahamas from Cape Canaveral.

The line's 2,600-passenger *Ecstasy* (which entered service in June 1991), sails on alternate Eastern and Western seven-day cruises to the Caribbean from Miami. The 70,000 ton *Sensation* launched in the fall of 1993. Another 70,000 ton ship, *Facination,* begins service in July 1994. Three more "Super Liners" are under construction.

Carnival appeals to all age groups, but no other line carries more cruisers between the ages of 20 and 50. Recently, the line also accelerated its onboard children's activities with "Camp Carnival," a program that keeps youngsters at various age levels busy from morning until night. Singles, honeymooners, and many families with children are seen on every Carnival cruise.

Carnival acquired Holland America Line and Windstar Cruises in 1989, both upscale lines that it operates and markets separately from the more middle-of-the-road and less expensive Carnival cruises. It has been through aggressive marketing and pricing as well as product that Carnival has managed to capture such a large percentage of cruise ship passengers.

CELEBRITY CRUISE LINES

Blue Lagoon Dr.
Suite 1000
Miami, FL 33126

Ships: Horizon, Meridian, Zenith.
Destinations: Bermuda, Caribbean, Panama Canal.
Description: Gourmet dining; fully equipped health club. Celebrity Cruises for the premium market, a casually elegant atmosphere; Fantasy Cruises, the value product, offers a festive atmosphere. The Celebrity fleet sails year-round to the Caribbean and Bermuda. The Fantasy fleet covers the Caribbean and Europe.

CELEBRITY CRUISES, with offices in New York and Miami, is the new upscale division of Chandris Lines, a Greek company with a history that dates back to 1915. Created in 1990, Celebrity Cruises operates quite separately from Chandris' traditional lower-priced Fantasy Cruises. To emphasize the distinction, the name Chandris no longer appears in either case.

In the post-World War II period, Chandris began operating regular sailings for the migrant and tourist trade between Britain, Greece, and Australia lasting until the late 1970s. In the interim, Chandris carried hundreds of thousands of Europeans to a new life "Down Under." In the Mediterranean, Chandris offered inexpensive cruises in small second-hand ships, proving to be a cost-effective way for tourists to visit many places in Greece and its islands in a short period of time. Gradually, the company renewed its fleet, always buying second-hand tonnage, and soon Chandris earned a reputation for being a very good value.

When Home Lines Cruises was sold, the Bermuda contact was up for bid, and Chandris created its Celebrity line to obtain the preferred sailing days and docking rights on Front Street in Hamilton and at St. George. Chandris successfully rebuilt the *Galileo* into the 1,106-passenger *Meridian,* and for the first time in its history, designed and built a brand-new ship, the 1,354 passenger *Horizon.* Late in 1991, a sister-ship, the *Zenith,* came on line to complete the Celebrity fleet. Three new ships are being built for Celebrity now.

As part of the upscale image, Michel Roux, Britain's best known French chef, acts as a consultant and supervises the menus aboard the three ships. Besides the dining, the entertainment, accommodations, and overall ambiance is distinctively upscale. The response to the new, higher-priced Celebrity Cruises has been overwhelmingly favorable, and Chandris has seemingly carved out a secure niche in the upscale market.

On the weekly warm-weather New York-based seven-day Bermuda cruises, the *Meridian* sails on Sundays to Hamilton for a mid-week, nearly four-day stay.

The *Horizon* sails onSaturdays for both Hamilton and St. George. With the ships as hotels, the line organizes an extensive program of sightseeing, sports, and beach activities.

In the winter, the *Meridian* and brand-new *Zenith* are based in Fort Lauderdale. The *Meridian* makes ten and eleven-day trips to Antigua, St. Thomas, and Nassau. The *Zenith* makes the same cruises on alternate weeks, operates to Ochos Rios, Grand Cayman, Playa del Carmen, and Cozumel at the same rates. The *Horizon is* based in San Juan for seven-day cruises to Martinique, Barbados, St. Lucia, Antigua, and St. Thomas.

CLUB MED

West 57th St.
New York,NY 10019

Ships: Club Med 1 and 2.
Destinations: Caribbean, Bali, Singapore.
Description: Luxury computer-controlled sailing ships with diving equipment, fitness center. Club Med's 615 -foot sleek sailing ships feature exotic itineraries, continental dining and activities; including complementary sports from the private marina and full gym. Seasonally, Club Med 1 sails the Caribbean and the Mediterranean; Club Med 2 sails in the Pacific from New Caledonia and Guam.

COSTA CRUISE LINES

Worls Trade Center
S.W. 8th Street
Miami, FL 33130-3097
358-7325

Ships: Costa Allegra, Costa Marina, Costa Classica, Costa Romantica, Daphne, Enricocosta, Eugeniocosta.
Destinations: Caribbean, Mediterranean, Northern Europe, Black Sea.
Description: Italian language classes, gelati stand, and pizzeria. Italian spirit makes a world of difference on the Costa Cruise Lines, featuring superb cuisine, peerless service, and luxurious European ambiance. Costa sails to ports in the Eastern, Western and Southern Caribbean, Alaska, Mediterranean, Black Sea and Holy Land.

COSTA CRUISE LINES N.V., based in Miami, FL, Will soon be adding three new vessels to its present four-ship fleet operating in the Caribbean. Its parent company, Genoa-based Costa Crociere S.P.A., also operates two ships in the Mediterranean and South America, as well as being involved in a joint venture called Prestige Cruises with Sovcomflot AKP of Moscow. One ship, the Danae has Prestige lable.

Costa's parade of new ships begins with the brand-new $325 million CostaClassica, a 1,350-passenger 50,000 grt ship that debuted in the Caribbean February 1, 1992. She will sail weeklong cruises on alternate Eastern and Western Caribbean itineraries from Port Everglade.

Then in 1993, the CostaRomantica, also 50,000 grt and carrying 1,350, joined the fleet with a still unannounced itinerary. The 810-passenger 30,000-grt CostaAllegra, sister ship to the slightly smaller CostaMarina (25,000-grt), went into service in October 1992, replacing the 420-passenger Daphne for seven-day Caribbean sailings.

The Costa Marina cruises the Mediterranean and North Africa in summer and offers alternate Eastern and Western Caribbean itineraries in the winter.

Costa Crociere operates the Eugenio Costa and the EnricoCosta in the Mediterranean in summer and South America in the winter. Primarily for European clientele.

COMMODORE CRUISE LINE

Douglas Rd. #600
Coral Gables, Fl 33134

Ships: Enchanted Seas.
Destinations: Eastern and Western Caribbean and the Mexican Riviera from New Orleans.
Description: Commodore offers cruises to popular destinations at an affordable price. Its mid-sized, classic ship features spacious, comfortable accommodations and attentive service.

COMMODORE CRUISE LINE, the North American holding of European shipping giant EffJohn International, is headquartered in Coral Cables, FL. The line, known for its "Happy Ships," offers an attractively priced, old-time cruise experience in up-to-date surroundings, on three classic, 1950s-era liners sailing North American itineraries.Another key strategy has been to base ships in seldom used, interesting ports like San Diego and New Orleans. The 736 passenger *Enchanted Seas is* now home-ported year-round at the latter, cruising a week long Western Caribbean/Mexico route. Specially priced pre and postcruise vacation packages are offered for all home ports.

CUNARD CROWN CRUISES

Box 10265
Riviera Beach, FL 33419

Ships: Cunard Countess, Cunard Princess, Cunard Crown Jewel, Cunard Crown Dynasty, Cunard Crown Monarch.
Destinations: Caribbean, Panama Canal, Canary Islands, Mediterranean, Alaska, South Pacific, Asian islands, Far East, East Coast Canada.
Destinations: Good value. Traditional, intimate ambience. 24-hour room service; special fitness menu. Crown has reintroduced a traditional, intimate shipboard experience, akin to the cruising style of the '60s and '70s, but with the advantage of new, state-of-the-art ships. The Crown Monarch ('90), Crown Jewel ('92), and Crown Dynasty ('93) sail to the eastern and western Caribbean, New England/Canada and the Panama Canal.

CUNARD LINE LTD., based in New York City and owned by Trafalgar House, London, England, pioneered the great era of trans-Atlantic steamship sailings way back in 1840. Ironically, the company now operates the sole surviving liner making regular Atlantic crossings, the *QE2*. Cunard is no late-comer to pleasure cruising, either, becoming well-established in this field in the 1920s. In 1949, the *Caronia*, known as the Green Goddess because of the four shades of green paint, became the world's first major purpose-built cruise ship.

Queen Mary, Queen Elizabeth, and *Mauritania* are names known to anyone interested in sea travel. Presently, the Cunard fleet numbers seven, and includes two ships of the former Norwegian America Cruises and two Sea Goddess ships.

The 1,880-passenger *Queen Elizabeth 2,* the last true transatlantic liner, divides her year between regular high-speed crossings between New York and England and France and cruises from New York and Southampton, England. In January, the *QE2* traditionally makes a long, three-month world cruise. In 1983 Cunard and British Airways began the innovative and hugely successful sea-air combination of the *QE2* and the Concorde supersonic airliner. Unique to the ship are five restaurants with allocation according to cabin category. The 790 passenger *Cunard Countess is* based in San Juan for seven-day Caribbean cruising, while the 750-passenger sister-ship *Cunard Princess* cruises from Europe to the Atlantic islands and in the Mediterranean. Both ships are aimed at the middle-market.

In 1983 Cunard bought the top-rated Norwegian American Cruises and its 588-passenger *Sagafjord* and 736-passenger *Vistafjord,* often regarded as the most luxurious pair of ships afloat. These two have the whole world as their oyster, and depending on the season, may be seen in the Caribbean, Mediterranean, Northern Europe, Alaska, the South Pacific, or Australia. Then in 1986 Cunard acquired the two Sea Goddess ships, a concept that offers the ultimate luxury in an intimate setting for only 116 passengers occupying one-room suites. Everything is included in the ticket price, and even tipping is discouraged. The *Sea Goddess I* and *Sea Goddess 11* cruise both the Eastern and Western Hemispheres.

CRYSTAL CRUISES

Avenue of the Stars
Suite 200
Los Angeles, CA 90067

Ship: Crystal Harmony, Crystal Symphony
Destinations: Caribbean, Panama Canal, Mediterranean, northern Europe, Black Sea, Holy Land, transatlantic, Canada, New England, South Pacific and South America.
Description: 3,000-square-foot ocean-view spa and beauty salon; Caesar's Palace at Sea casino, ethnic restaurants. Crystal's Five-Stars-Plus ship, Crystal Harmony, offers 960 discriminating travelers a luxurious cruise experience filled with first-class accommodations. Crystal Cruises offers a variety of cruises from 10 to 88 days to Europe, Trans-canal and the Pacific/Orient.

First Class!

CUNARD LINE

Fifth Avenue
New York, NY 10017-2453
880-7500

Ships: Sagafjord, Vistafjord. Sea Goddess I, Sea Goddess II.

Destinations: All over the world; transatlantic and world cruises. Amazon River, Far East, southern Caribbean, Mediterranean.

Description: Complimentary champagne and caviar. Large picture windows, roomy cabins. Ships include the Queen Elizabeth 2, the white-glove service of the Sagafjord and Vistafjord, yacht-like ambiance on the Sea Goddess I and II and the four-star Countess and Princess. More than 300 ports in 1993, including world cruises, Transatlantic, Alaska, Caribbean, Mediterranean, Baltic, Black Sea, South Pacific, Canary Islands and Europe.

DELTA QUEEN STEAMBOAT COMPANY

Suite 30 Robin Street Wharf
New Orleans, LA 70130

Ships: Delta Queen, Mississippi Queen.
Destinations: Mississippi, Arkansas, Ohio, Cumberland, and Tennessee rivers.
Description: Authentic paddle wheelers with Victorian-style lounges. River cruising in the gracious style and leisurely pace of an earlier era aboard America's last overnight paddle-wheel steamboats. Rediscover the wilderness of the upper Mississippi, the Ohio River's scenic villages and the Deep South of ante-bellum plantations and Civil War battlefields.

DELTA QUEEN STEAMBOAT CO., based in New Orleans, LA, is a microcosm of America itself with its two steamboats, the 176-passenger *Delta Queen* and the 400-passenger *Mississippi Queen.* Mark Twain could easily have been describing them when he said, "The steamboats are finer than anything onshore. Compared with superior dwelling-houses and first-class hotels, they were indubitably magnificent, they were palaces."

Throughout the year, on the Mississippi, the Ohio, the Tennessee, and the Cumberland rivers, Delta Queen offers two 12-night cruises with an incredible variety of themes from "The Great Steamboat Race" to "The Old South," from "Wilderness Rivers" to "Crossroads of America." From New Orleans to as far north as St. Paul, as far northeast as Pittsburgh, and as far east as Nashville and Chattanooga, the two stern paddle wheelers churn against time and currents to recreate the great steamboat days of the 1800s.

It is Dixieland jazz, ante-bellum moods, fried catfish, calliopes, Creole dishes, grits, and costume parties. But it is also modern comfort, a wide variety of entertainment, excellent food, attentive service, and just plain fun for all as the panorama of America passes ever so slowly. The 150-year-old traditions are mixed with state-of-the-art conveniences from air-conditioning to a swimming pool (on the *Mississippi Queen).*

The polished brass, etched-glass, gleaming mahogany, and velvet coverings all set the scene on both steamboats. The smaller *Delta Queen* (built in 1925) is a true relic from the past and has been declared a national treasure. The *Mississippi Queen* went into service in 1976.

Delta Queen Steamboat Co. cruises depart from New Orleans, Memphis, St. Louis, St. Paul, Cincinnati, Pittsburgh, Nashville, Louisville, and Chattanooga. Each of the steamboats has eight cabin categories that range from the Captain's Veranda Suites to inside cabins. All cabins on both boats have private facilities, but, it must be noted, there are cabins on the *Mississippi Queen* that have obstructed river views.

All cruises can start or end with well-conceived "Steamboatin's Port City Vacations" that include first-class hotel accommodations, sightseeing, baggage transfers, and some meals. Special round-trip airfares are available through the " Steamboatin' Plus Air" program. Steamboat people yearly create special theme cruises such as "Fall Foliage" and "Big Bands," and tie in with such special events as the Kentucky Derby.

DIAMOND CRUISE LINE

Concorde Centre
NE 191st St.
Suite 304
North Miami Beach, FL 33180
932-3388

Ship: SSC Radisson Diamond.

Destinations: Bahamas, Caribbean, Mediterranean, Trans-Atlantic, Trans-Panama.

Description: Noted for its superior stability, the twin-hulled offers luxury accommodations, 5-star dining, top-notch entertainment and exciting destinations.

RADISSON DIAMOND is a twin-hull cruise ship that was launched May 1992, marking the cruise debut of Radisson Hotels International. The 350-passenger ship is designed to serve the upscale segment of the cruise market. Its innovative design diminishes pitch, roll and heave movements to maximize comfort and quality.

The RADISSON DIAMOND prides itself in complete facilities for corporate conferences and incentive groups, including telecommunications and publishing equipment, and meeting rooms with state-of-the-art video and sound systems. It is the first luxury cruise liner to be fitted with an eight-channel satellite system to handle a high volume of telephone, data and fax calls. In addition, guests dine at their own convenience, enjoy the European-style spa with its diamond-mine theme, and highly personalized service.

DOLPHIN CRUISE LINE

S. America Way
Miami, FL 33132

Ships: Dolphin IV, Seabreeze, Oceanbreeze.
Destinations: Bahamas, Caribbean, Mexico, Trans-Panama.
Description: Nice, older ships, award-winning cuisine, gracious white-glove service, friendly crew and staff, exotic ports, endless activities. 3 and 4 night cruises to Nassau and Key West, 7 and 14 night cruises to the eastern/western Caribbean and the Panama Canal, Southern Caribbean from Aruba.

A fine economy cruise line, great value for a very low price. Best deal. Not fancy, just good service, excellent food and comfortable ships.

EPIROTIKI LINES

Fifth Av.
Suite 605
New York, NY 10176

Ships: Jason, Neptune, Odysseus, Orpheus, Pallas Athena, Triton, World Renaissance.
Destinations: Caribbean, Mediterranean, Red Sea, River (South America, Europe), Russia, Trans-Atlantic.
Description: As a destination-oriented cruise line, Epirotiki focuses on a variety of exotic ports of call. The largest and oldest operator of cruises in the Mediterranean, operating 11 ships. Greek Isles, Mediterranean, Black Sea, Caribbean, Red Sea and Transatlantic cruises.

FANTASY CRUISES

Blue Lagoon Dr.
Suite 1000
Miami, FL 33126

Ships: Amerikanis, Britanis.
Destinations: Caribbean, Mediterranean, Black Sea, northern Europe, transatlantic.
Description: Gym, health club, Las Vegas-style casino.

FANTASY CRUISES, a Chandris Cruises Inc. division headquartered in Miami, FL, represents the culmination of a rich maritime tradition that goes back to the prejetage days of long-distance ocean travel. With the advent of its Celebrity Cruises (see separate profile), Chandris is now carrying this tradition to the upscale market.

Founded in 1915, Chandris entered the Europe/Australia trade in 1959 in direct competition with two venerable British shipping firms, P&O and Orient Line. The challenge was so spirited that the two British lines were forced to air-condition their ships and to put better vessels into one-class service on this and other worldwide routes.

The Chandris policy over the years has been to buy good older ships and then give to them amenities that make them as good as or better than the newer competition. From 1992 the vessels of Fantasy Cruises (the banner under which the companies budgetpriced cruise ships now sail) reflect the grace and deep-water seaworthiness of an earlier era and, at the same time, offer the modern amenities expected by today's cruise passenger.

Each ship has its own personality. Best seaboat in the fleet, as well as one of the oldest and most popular, is the *Britanis,* built in 1932 as Matson Line's *Monterey.* Most of the year she sails from Miami on two-night cruises to Nassau, and five-night trips to Key West and Mexico. But each fall she sails on a cruise of about 50 days from Miami around South America. These have been so successful that the line has considered sending her farther afield. The 623-passenger *Amerikanis* offers seven-day cruises from San Juan to the Caribbean year-round. She began life in 1952 as the British Union Castle liner *Kenya Castle* on a regular service completely circumnavigating Africa. She still displays quaint evidence of her British heritage. The *Victoria,* accommodating 550, joins the *Amerikanis* on week long winter trips from San Juan, then sails in European waters during the summer. She joins the 686-berth former car-ferry *Azur,* which has recently been Europe-based throughout the year. The *Victoria,* which entered service in 1936 (also in the Union Castle around Africa service), was so thoroughly rebuilt in the 1950s for the Incres Line that she now looks more Italian than British and is a ship of special charm. The North American ships, wherever they sail, normally offer cruise-only fares starting at under $100 per day (less than $130 per day with air arrangements).

In addition to these low rates, what has made Fantasy Cruises so popular? Cuisine far better than most other companies in the lower price range, thanks to Apollo Ship Chandlers of Miami, caterer for ships; good entertainment, which has been a company hallmark almost since the line's founding; vessels that are well cared-for; and innovative itineraries and cruise lengths.

HOLLAND AMERICA LINE

Elliot Av. West
Seattle, WA 98119

Ships: Maasdam, Nieuw Amsterdam, Noordam, Statendam, Westerdam, Rotterdam.
Destinations: All over the world with extended world cruises.
Description: Hospitable Indonesian staff. Passage to Fitness program; low-calorie menu. High-value premium cruises offering a 120-year heritage of Dutch seamanship, impeccable service, spacious staterooms.

HOLLAND AMERICA LINE, established in 1871 and now based in Seattle, WA, is famous not only for the trans-Atlantic service it maintained for a hundred years but also for the cruises it has offered for most of this century. The 1938-built, twin funneled *Nieuw Amsterdam* was not only an aristocrat of the Atlantic, but also a familiar sight throughout the Mediterranean and Caribbean for most of her long career. The current *Rotterdam* made a world cruise almost every year for a quarter-century.

Fans of Holland America admire the company for retaining so many of the civilized touches that add to the romance of ocean travel-fresh flowers everywhere, music of a violin trio at dinner, fine cuisine and decor, ships that display a deep-water grace, smiling Indonesian and Filipino staff-members, and everything in good taste. (Filipino crew in cocktail lounges and Indonesian staff in dining room and for cabin stewards.)

The line added the new 1,214-passenger sisters *Nieuw Amsterdam* and *Noordam* in 1983 and 1984, and the 1,476 passenger *Westerdam* in 1988 (formerly Home Line's *Homeric,* but "stretched" to accommodate this number of passengers). Also during the previous decade, Holland America acquired Westours, the largest tour/cruise-tour operator in Alaska, and became a major player in cruises and tours to Alaska.

Purchase of the line by Carnival Cruise Lines in January 1989 gave HAL capital to build new ships and the money not only to maintain its standards but also to take chances for instance, to re-enter the long cruise market. The first of these, a 'Round South America cruise by the *Rotterdam* in 1990, astonished everyone by virtually selling out in advance of any major publicity. In 1992, the flagship will sail to the Orient, to Rio, around Hawaii, and to many other destinations.

The three other HAL vessels will offer numerous sailings to the Caribbean in winter, Alaska in summer, trans-Panama Canal positioning cruises in between, and occasional extended cruises.

Three new vessels are now being built by one of Italy's premier builders of great passenger ships Fincantieri in Trieste. The 50,000 grt, 250-passenger *Statendam, Maasdam,* and *Ryndam* entered service in 1992, 1993, and 1994 respectively. They will be the finest vessels ever to bear these traditional Holland America names. They will combine lovely interiors with more than a hint of the graceful, patrician lines of their predecessors. The trio will be suitable for both long-distance and shorter cruises.

Holland America fares vary widely according to season and route, but are in the middle price range.

IVARIAN LINES

Ships: Americana.
Destination: Buenos Aires.
Description: Freighter with 48 large, fully equipped cabins.

MAJESTY CRUISE LINE

South America Way
Miami, FL 33132-2073
358-5122
Ships: Royal Majesty.
Destination: Bahamas, Mexico.
Description: Quality, grace, taste and casual elegance are what you will experience when you embark on a journey aboard the new Royal Majesty.

NORWEGIAN CRUISE LINE

Merrick Way
Coral Gables, FL 33134

Ships: Starward, Southward, Dreamward, Seaward, Westward, Windward, Norway.
Destinations: Caribbean and Catalina Islands, Bermuda, Mexican Riviera, Alaska.
Description: Themed supersport cruises; excellent entertainment; children's program. Norwegian Cruise Line operates a fleet of seven ships and is the official cruise line of the NFL, NBA, Basketball Hall of Fame and Universal Studios in Florida and Hollywood.

NORWEGIAN CRUISE LINE, a subsidiary of Kloster Cruise Ltd., is headquartered in Coral Gables, FL. Known as Norwegian Caribbean Lines when it was formed in 1966, NCL was the pioneer of today's seven-day, informal but luxurious cruises from Miami to the Caribbean.

The company was originally founded by Knut Kloster of Norway and Ted Arison who, in the early 1970s, broke away to form Carnival Cruise Lines. From one ship, the original *Sunward,* NCL expanded from 1968 to 1971 to include the 758 passenger *Starward,* the 730-passenger *Skyward,* and the 752 passenger *Southward.* These three ships established one-class, upscale but affordable seven- and 14-day cruises from Miami to the Bahamas and Caribbean, which led to today's modern cruise industry and established the Port of Miami as the number one cruise port in the world.

In 1977 NCL acquired the former *Cunard Adventurer,* renamed and refitted her as the 676-passenger *Sunward 11,* and launched a revolutionary concept known as "Bahamarama." In addition to the traditional ports of Nassau and Freeport, this was the first three- and four-day cruise to the Bahamas utilizing a small deserted island as a stop.

In i980 NCL took a giant step by acquiring the former transatlantic liner *France,* refurbishing her for $140 million and renaming her the *Norway.* With the addition of two new decks and 135 cabins in 1990, the 2,044-passenger ship regained the title of largest cruise ship in the world, after having lost it to RCCL's *Sovereign of the Seas* in the late 1980s.

Kloster Cruise acquired Royal Viking Line in 1984, adding three more ships to the company fleet. One of RVL's ships, the *Royal Viking Star* was renamed as the 790-passenger *Westward* and incorporated into the NCL fleet in early 1991. Another, the *Royal Viking Sky,* was transferred to NCL and renamed *Sunward* late last year, as majority interest in the *Sunwardll* was sold to Epirotiki, who renamed the latter the*Triton.* Meanwhile, NCL also added a brand-new ship, the 1,534-passenger *Seaward,* to its ranks in 1988. NCL's fleet now totals seven ships which call at more than 25 ports in the Bahamas, Mexico, Caribbean, Bermuda, Southern California, and the Mexican Riviera.

NCL has maintained a leading role in the industry with a series of innovative marketing programs as well as an extensive variety of itineraries, entertainment, and activities appealing to a diversified segment of upscale vacationers including families, professionals, and special interest groups. Most veteran cruisers consider the *Norway* the best ship afloat for live entertainment.

OCEANIC CRUISES

West Century Blvd.
Suite 390
Los Angeles, CA

Ships: Oceanic.
Destinations: Specializes in cruises to the Orient, Concentrates on Japan, plus mainland China, Korea and eastern Russia.
Description:

OCEAN CRUISE LINES, a part of the Paris, France, based Paquet Group, operates a small, first-class vessel, mainly for North American passengers, that roves European and South American waters on a variety of extended popular and off-beat itineraries. Its U.S. headquarters in Fort Lauderdale, FL, conducts sales and marketing; operations are handled in Paris. Paquet also owns Paquet French Cruises and Pearl Cruises.

Paquet acquired Ocean and its sister company, Pearl Cruises, in mid-1990 from a Swiss conglomerate that had formed the original two-ship line in 1983 as an adjunct to a tour operations business. Paquet is jointly owned by Chargeurs, a major French conglomerate, and Accor, the largest international hospitality company.

Ocean's basic policy has been to stay with small ships, provide a high level of service, and follow itineraries that appeal to the intellectually curious. This approach has attracted a steady stream of middle-to-high-income Americans, ages 45 to 75, who have cruised extensively and enjoy foreign cultures and experiences as much as cruising itself. Since joining Paquet, small numbers of French and British also are among the passengers, but Ocean's (and Pearl's) president Robert Iversen assures that the line will not deviate from its American orientation.

Cabins are available in 12 categories; cruise-only per-diem rates on a typical sailing average $225 (per. pers./dbl. occ.), but more than 70 percent of the passengers buy a heavily promoted, all-inclusive "CruiseTour" package, that includes air/sea costs and pre and post-cruise hotel stays.

ORIENT LINES

Ship: Marco Polo.
Destinations: Africa, Mideast, Antarctica, South Pacific, Southeast Asia, Australia, China, Japan.
Description: Health clubs. Imaginative menu. Celebrity lecturers.

PAQUET CRUISES

N.W. 5th Way, Suite 4000
Fort Lauderdale, FL 33309
772-8600 or (800) 556-8850
Ships: Mermoz, Pearl.
Destinations: Africa, Antarctica, Australia, Bali, Caribbean, China, eastern Europe, Egypt, Far East, Galapagos. India, Japan, Mediterranean, Russia, Scandinavia, South America and Vietnam.
Description: Includes Pearl Cruises and Ocean Cruise Lines. Offers exotic itineraries for sophisticated travelers. Ships for 450+ passengers feature outstanding cuisine and service.

PAQUET FRENCH CRUISES, represented in this country by its subsidiary, Ocean Cruise Lines of Ft. Lauderdale, FL, was originally one of the steamship companies established in the last century to link France with its overseas possessions. As early as 1860, Paquet operated a number of specialized passenger and cargo services in the Mediterranean, soon expanding down the African coast. The line is now part of the Paris-based French conglomerate, Chargeurs S.A., owners of Sofitel and Novotel, and currently operates under its own house flag and colors the 13,804-grt 580-passenger *Mermoz* .

The *Mermoz is* a colorful and fascinating ship that provides a change-of-pace from all other cruise vessels. She is now the only conventional French cruise ship in operation. On her worldwide itineraries, she offers such amenities as fine French cuisine, one sitting dining, and friendly, sophisticated service. Crew-members are predominantly French, although there are Indonesian dining room and cabin stewards. Cuisine and service are upscale, while the accommodations are comfortable but unpretentious.

Built in 1957 for the Fabre Line as the *Jean Mermoz* (named for the famous French aviator), the vessel was transferred to Paquet in 1965. As recently as the mid-'60s, she maintained a regular four-class passenger and cargo service between Marseilles and African ports. Occasionally, she was used on pleasure cruises. In 1970 she was converted into a full-time cruise ship, and her name was shortened to the *Mermoz.*

The *Mermoz* generally cruises the waters of Northern Europe and the Mediterranean in summer and, during early fall, provides the setting for the famed Music Festival at Sea. For French-speaking theater-lovers, there is also the Theater Festival at Sea, with performances of outstanding French plays. Variety is the hallmark of her routings. In 1991 there was a total immersion Berlitz French Language cruise. This winter she sails the Caribbean and Mexican Riviera, touching at some ports not normally included in these familiar waters.

Public rooms are a floating tribute to the French

maritime heritage with models of such French liners as *L'Atlantique, Ancerille,* and *Massilia.* Corridors are lined with framed posters and first-rate photos from the Chargeurs Collection. Then there is the ship herself: teak decks, sheer, and pleasantly nautical areas for sunbathing and strolling. Cabins are basic- adequate but lacking in the ambiance of the rest of the ship.

Fares vary greatly by cruise and season. Fares for theme cruises are higher but, especially in the case of the Music Festival at Sea, this does not keep them from selling out far in advance.

PREMIER CRUISE LINES

Challenger Rd.
Cape Canaveral, FL 32920

Ships: Atlantic, Oceanic, Majestic.
Destinations: Bahamas.
Description: Kids' program. Appearances by Looney Tunes, Bugs Bunny and friends, characters beginning April 1. Bahamas, combination cruise and Walt Disney World vacation.

The Official Cruise Line of Walt Disney World offers the best family and children's programs, with exclusive appearances from the famous Disney characters on board every cruise. The No. 1 family cruise line combines a 3 or 4 night Bahamas cruise to Nassau Lucaya Freeport, Cozumel-Cancun and Key West, with vacations to Disney World and other central Florida attractions.

PREMIER CRUISE LINES, the Official Cruise Line of Walt Disney World, was created in 1984, and its three "Big Red Boats" offer three-day cruises, four-day cruises, and seven-day cruise and Disney vacations. Sailings are to the Bahamas from the line's base, Port Canaveral, 50 miles east of Orlando, FL. Ships include the 1,500-passenger Star/Ship *Oceanic,* the 1,600 passenger *StarShip Atlantic,* and the 950-passenger *StarShip.Majestic.* All have been modified to accommodate additional passengers in upper bunks and to provide special entertainment areas for children.

Premier offers one of the most unusual and entertaining vacation packages for families. The cruise-Disney combination week includes: either three or four cruise days; either four or three days in a hotel near or at Walt Disney World; a three-day pass to the Magic Kingdom, Epcot Center, and Disney-MGM Studios; a tour of Spaceport USA at Kennedy Space Center; and a rental car with unlimited mileage.

From a welcome by Disney characters such as Mickey, Minnie, and Goofy to fun-filled entertainment aboard and a super beach party, the cruises are all designed for the maximum enjoyment of parents and their offspring. The young people are separated into age categories (24, 5-7, 8-12, and teens) so their interests do not overlap. There are also special menus for all.

Premier has spent millions on two private Bahamian islands: Salt Cay near Nassau and Great Guana Cay in the Abacos. Here, the beach parties, plus the watersports, barbecues, and entertainment, offer a myriad of activities (or inactivities) for all ages.

There is the choice of three ships and four itineraries. The *Oceanic* leaves Port Canaveral every Friday, stays in Nassau from 1:30 p.m. Saturday to 6 a.m. Sunday, spends the rest of Sunday at Salt Cay, and returns to Port Canaveral Monday for sailing on the four-day cruise that afternoon. The four-day cruise adds a full day at sea. The *Atlantic* follows the same itinerary. The *Majestic* leaves on her three-day cruise on Friday, spending two days at Great Guana Cay, with optional tours to other Abacos islands; the four-day cruise, leaving on Sunday, has an added day at sea.

PRINCESS CRUISES

Santa Monica Blvd.
Los Angeles. Ca 90067

Ships: Star Princess, Regal Princess, Crown Princess, Royal Princess, Sky Princess, Golden Princess, Fair Princess, Island Princess, Pacific Princess.
Destinations: Caribbean, Mexico, Alaska, Black Sea, Scandinavia/Russia, Mediterranean, South America, South Pacific, Hawaii, India/Holy Land, Transcanal, Asia/Orient and Canada /New England.
Description: Unusually spacious cabins; youth program; fitness program. The famous Love Boat fleet features richly appointed, spacious ships, where passengers experience warm, personal treatment, fine dining and exciting entertainment.

PRINCESS CRUISES, one of the world's largest cruise lines, is based in Los Angeles, CA. From a modest beginning with a 6,000-grt ferry vessel called the *Princess Patricia,* the company pioneered cruises to the Mexican Riviera in 1965-66.

The name "Princess" stuck as the company began chartering other ships, including a Norwegian ship it renamed the *Island Princess* in 1972. Acquisition of Princess Cruises by the London based Peninsular & Oriental Steam Navigation Company Inc. in 1974 combined the marketing savvy and success of Princess with the resources, history, and tradition of P&O. By 1975 the line had not only established a modern fleet but also a name instantly recognizable as star of the TV series "The Love Boat."

The series gave a giant boost to a fledgling new pleasure cruise industry in general, although no one benefited more than Princess itself. The 20,000-grt 610-passenger *Island Princess* was joined by her sister, the *Pacific Princess* (they had been Flagship Lines' *Island Venture* and *Sea Venture,* respectively). During the same period P&O added its ship *Spirit of London* to the Princess fleet as the *Sun Princess* (later sold to Premier).

In 1984 P&O also transferred its 710-passenger *Sea Princess* over to Princess Cruises (but took her back last year), and the line added the first of several new, large, luxurious ships, the 1,200 passenger *Royal Princess.* Subsequent new ships came as a direct result of Princess' major acquisition of Sitmar Cruises in 1988, an Italian company which at the time owned three ships with three new ships on order.

Today, largely because of that acquisition, Princess has a fleet of nine ships and is building the largest passenger ship in the world. Besides the two "Love Boat" sisters, *Island Princess* and *Pacific Princess,* along with the *Royal Princess,* the fleet consists of the 1,200-passenger *Sky Princess,* 1,470 passenger *Star Princess,* and two more sets of sisters: the 890 passenger *Fair Princess* and the 1,590 passenger *Crown Princess* and *Regal Princess.* The two latter ships were inaugurated in 1990 and 1991 respectively.

REGENCY CRUISES

Ships: Regent Rainbow, Regent Sea, Regent Star, Regent Sun, Regent Spirit.

Destinations: Caribbean, Panama Canal, Central America, South America, Alaska, Hawaii, New England, eastern Canada, Mediterranean, Black Sea.

Description: Unusual itineraries at affordable rates. Healthy menu; children's program. It is distinguished by European-style service, continental cuisine and a casually elegant atmosphere.

REGENCY CRUISES is a six-year-old privately owned line, by Captain Anthony Lelakis headquartered in New York City. Its three ships, all built between 1957 and 1964 as ocean liners, are similar in size and passenger capacity and provide a gracious, quality cruising experience.

Regency's first vessel, the 22,000-grt 760-passenger *Regent Sea,* was quickly successful, and in less than two years was joined by the 24,500-grt 950-passenger *Regent Star,* and by the 25,500-grt 836-passenger *Regent Sun* about a year after that. The Regent Spirit is a small, 400 passenger ship with all outside cabins. The line's progress reflects a basic three-fold strategy: providing an affordable quality cruising experience that includes amenities usually spent on higher-priced cruises; using ships of a size that permit both extensive facilities and an intimate atmosphere- and sailing innovative itineraries.

Regency offers a classic cruise product in an informal atmosphere, tending toward the casual, spacious, nicely appointed cabins and public rooms, and European-style service. The dining room emphasizes fine food prepared in the classic French manner, but with a lighter touch. Menus also include regional specialties and dishes for dieters and vegetarians.

To broaden its passenger base middle-income Americans in the 40- to 60-year-old age group who have cruised previously, packages were introduced last year to attract honeymooners, single parents and grandparents and their offsprings, young families and large family groups. A limited gentleman host program, started in 1990, proved popular with single women seeking social companionship and was recently expanded.

Varying itineraries have helped lure a high percentage of repeat passengers. For the current winter/spring season, each ship was deployed for the first time in a different port for seven day Caribbean sailings. The *Regent Sun* covers southern islands from San Juan; the *Regent Sea,* out of Tampa, calls at western ports and Mexico; and the *Regent Star* touches South America and nearby islands, and makes a Regency-pioneered partial transit of the Panama Canal, sailing from Montego Bay.

In May the *Regent Sea* and *Regent Star* make trans-Canal cruises to Alaska for a summer series of weekly, one-way sailings from Vancouver to Whittier. The *Regent Star* then repositions to the Caribbean, and the *Regent Sea* starts her annual circumnavigation of South America, from Los Angeles to Tampa. This nearly two-month voyage also is sold in segments. The *Regent Sun* spends summer and early fall on a seven-day/ one-way New York/Montreal route that highlights New England, French Canada, and the Maritime Provinces.

RENAISSANCE CRUISES

Eller Dr. # 300
Ft. Lauderdale, FL 33335-0307
2601

Ships: Renaissance I-IV, Renaissance V-VIII.

Destinations: Caribbean, Mediterranean, northern Europe, Baltic, Africa, Seychelles, Asian islands, Far East.

Description: 114 guests, all outside suites, no tux, no tie, no ice sculptures. All-suite vessels, many with private balconies.

ROYAL CARIBBEAN CRUISE LINE

Caribbean Way
Miami, FL 33132

Ships: Sun Viking, Song of Norway, Nordic Prince, Song of America, Viking Serenade, Nordic Empress, Sovereign of the Seas, Monarch of the Seas, Majesty of the Seas.
Destinations: Bahamas and Ensenada, Bermuda, Caribbean, Panama Canal, Mexican Riviera, Alaska, Pacific Coast, Mediterranean, northern Europe, Baltic.
Description: Dozens of activities; excellent entertainment; children's program. Royal Caribbean has become the world's largest cruise brand by building on its reputation for award-winning service, spectacular modern ships, excellent cuisine, high-caliber entertainment and value. The Bahamas, Bermuda, Caribbean, Panama Canal, Mexico, Alaska, Mediterranean, British Isles, Baltic, North Cape/ Norwegian fjords, Greek Isles, Scandinavia/ Russia, Africa and the Canary Islands.

ROYAL CARIBBEAN CRUISES LTD., headquartered in the company's Port of Miami, FL, office building, has consistently received awards and accolades from passengers who have sailed on the line's widespread itineraries that include Bermuda, the Caribbean, Mexico, and Alaska.

Founded in 1969 as Royal Caribbean Cruise Line by three prominent Norwegian shipping companies, the company merged with Admiral Cruises in 1988 as a new privately owned holding company. RCCL's first ship, the

1,022-passenger *Song of Norway,* entered service in 1970, followed by the 1,022 passenger *Nordic Prince* the next year. The two ships were lengthened and rebuilt in 1978 and 1980 respectively.

Today the line has eight ships. The 726-passenger *Sun Viking,* ,1,390-passenger *Song of America,* 1,514-passenger *Viking Serenade,* 2,282-passenger *Sovereign of the Seas,* 1,610-passenger *Nordic Empress* and the brand new 2,354-passenger *Monarch of the Seas,* which began service last November, round out the list.

A sister ship to the latter, called *Majesty of the Seas, is* under construction and scheduled to enter service this May.

While there is no particular passenger profile, Royal Caribbean cruises generally appeal to couples in their 30s to 50s, family vacationers, honeymooners, and golfers (the line is the official line of the Professional Golf Assn. and offers golf to passengers in the Caribbean and Bermuda).

Throughout its 20-year history, RCCL has enjoyed one of the highest passenger satisfaction levels and repeat business of any cruise line. Service, food, and activities are top-rate, and the ships are run as luxury resorts. The ships are also instantly recognizable by a "Viking Crown Lounge," a cocktail and observation lounge built onto the rear funnel.

RCCL's seven-, eight-, and 10-night cruises cover

virtually every island in the Caribbean, with departures from Miami and San Juan, and include calls at the company's private beach, CocoCay in the Bahamas. The *Nordic Empress,* launched in June 1990, was designed specifically for the three- and four-day cruise to the Bahamas from Miami. Both the *Sovereign of the Seas* and the *Nordic Empress* have a dramatic nine-deck atrium or "Centrum," a focal point connecting many of the public rooms and separating them from cabin areas.

ROYAL CRUISE LINE

Maritime Plaza
Suite 1400
San Francisco , CA 94111

Ships: Crown Odyssey, Royal Odyssey, Star Odyssey.
Destinations: 7-28 day cruise vacations to the Orient, Africa, China, Scandinavia, British Isles, Canaries, Mediterranean, Alaska, Panama Canal, Hawaii, Canada/New England, Amazon, Caribbean, Mexico and Colonial America.
Description: Predominantly mature clientele. Fitness centers; low-calorie menu. Superb itineraries and outstanding values in deluxe cruising for mature travelers. Gentlemen hosts for dancing, alternative heart-healthy cuisine and award-winning, friendly Greek service.

ROYAL CRUISE LINE, headquartered in San Francisco, CA, is a wholly-owned subsidiary of Kloster Cruise Ltd., an old-line Norwegian shipping firm that also owns Norwegian Cruise Line and Royal Viking Line. Royal offers an upscale experience on three deluxe ships that sail extended, worldwide itineraries.

Kloster acquired Royal in 1989 from founder Pericles S. Panagopoulos, whose Greek company launched its first vessel in 1974, the then-new 10,500-grt *Golden Odyssey.* The San Francisco office was established the same year, and developed a solid following for her, initially from the lucrative West Coast market. When the former

Doric, renamed *Royal Odyssey,* joined the fleet in 1982, she also became a favorite, but was sold in 1988 after the new 34,250-grt *Crown Odyssey* arrived to earn her own raves. The esteem loyalists held for the *Royal Odyssey* prompted that name to be given the line's latest addition, the 28,000-grt former *Royal Viking Sea,* a transfer from RVL that began Royal service last December after a $20-million makeover.

Royal attracts affluent, experienced travelers with time for long cruises by delivering an extremely high level of personal service in luxurious settings, together with a wide choice of destinations. These are mainly people over 55, from many parts of the U. S. One measure of Royal's success is a 40 to 45 percent repeat passenger rate. Each sailing also attracts a large percentage of single women, many of whom come to enjoy the companionship of male hosts, who participate in a program Royal pioneered 10 years ago. Other popular innovations are the "New Beginnings" self-improvement series and a "Dine- to Your Heart's Content" menu, developed with the American Heart Assn.

Each ship offers a comparable onboard experience, but each also offers something different. The 460-passenger *Golden Odyssey* is low-key and intimate; the 1,052 passenger *Crown Odyssey is* noted for her roomy, comfortable cabins and outstanding public areas; the new 765-passenger *Royal Odyssey is* a blend of both and has a single-sitting dining room.

Most itineraries range from 10 to more than 20 days. In 1992 the *Royal Odyssey* sails Orient, Africa, and South Pacific routes, as well as Alaska, Canada/New England, Hawaii, and the Mexican Riviera. Following Caribbean and Mexican Riviera schedules, the *Golden Odyssey* cruises the Mediterranean, before sailing 27 days from Athens to Singapore. The *Crown Odyssey* cruises the Mexican Riviera, Hawaii, South America, Mediterranean, and Scandinavia.

ROYAL VIKING LINE

Merrick Way
Coral Gables, FL, 33134

Ships: Royal Viking Sun, Royal Viking Queen.
Destinations: Caribbean, Panama Canal, Mediterranean, northern Europe, Baltic, transatlantic, extended world tours.
Description: Cuisine by master chefs. Innovative World Affairs program. Royal Viking Line has an unparalleled reputation for elegance, dining and service, These ships have defined a quality of cruising that transcends time. Sailing 6 to 97 days, calling on India, Scandinavia/Russia, South America, Africa, Canada/New England, the Mediterranean and the Orient.

SEABOURN CRUISE LINE

Francisco St.
San Francisco, CA 94133

Ships: Seabourn Pride, Seabourn Spirit.
Destinations: Amazon, Panama Canal and the Caribbean. New England/Canada, Transatlantic, Mediterranean, Europe/Baltic/Scandinavia, the Far East.
Description: The ultimate cruise experience for discriminating clientele. Each room is a suite, and cuisine and service are unmatched. Earned the 1992 Conde Nast Traveller "Readers' Choice Award" for the best cruise line in the world. Huge cabins.

SEAWIND CRUISE LINE

Coral Way
Miami, FL 33145

Ships: Seawind Crown.
Destination: Southern Caribbean.
Description: The 624 - passenger tss Seawind Crown, a nice, older ship, features spaciousness, quality cuisine and an international atmosphere that has helped make Seawind America's most successful new line. The tss Seawind Crown sails every Sunday on a 7 - night southern Caribbean cruise. International cuisine; kid's program.

SEVEN SEAS CRUISE LINE

Market Street, Suite 2600
San Francisco, CA 94105-2102
285-1835

Ships: Song of Flower.

Destinations: Red Sea, Indian Ocean, Far East, Asian islands, Mediterranean, Black Sea, northern Europe, Baltic.

Description: 144 staff members for 172 guests; gym. Provides a Five Star Plus cruise experience for a maximum of 172 guests. Small-ship luxury, personalized service and exceptional all-inclusive value.

STAR CLIPPERS

Ships: Star Flyer, Star Clipper.
Destinations: Caribbean, Mediterranean.
Description: New, unique clipper ships. Library with fireplace.

SUN LINE CRUISES

Rockefeller Plaza
Suite 315
New York, NY 10020

Ships: Stella Solaris, Stella Oceanis, Stella Maris.
Destinaitons: Caribbean, Amazon, Panama Canal, transatlantic.
Description: Unusual itineraries. Family-owned and operated line offering unique itineraries and on-board ambiance of casual elegance. Enrichment programs, cabaret-style entertainment and European service. April-October: Italy, Greek Islands, Turkey, Egypt and Israel. December-April: Caribbean, Panama Canal, Amazon River and South America.

WINDSTAR CRUISES

Elliott Av.
West Seattle, WA 98119

Ships: Wind Star, Wind Song, Wind Spirit.
Destinations: Caribbean, Mediterranean, French Polynesia, Thailand, Malaysia.
Description: Luxury four-masted sailing ships with computer controls; informal. Windstar's extraordinary four-masted cruise ships pamper 148 guests with exceptional service, unregimented activities, spacious accommodations and high-tech sailing. Three high-tech, luxury sail cruise ships offer 7 day itineraries in the Mediterranean, Caribbean, and Virgin Islands, and year-round in French Polynesia and Southeast Asia.

WINDSTAR CRUISES, founded in 1984, was the first company to feature sail-powered cruise ships. The *Wind Star* (built in 1986), *Wind Song* (1987), and *Wind Spirit* (1988) have computer monitored and directed sailing systems, with diesel-electric backup propulsion. All carry 148 passengers, are 440-feet long, and have four passenger decks. They have Bahamian registry, and officers are primarily Norwegian and Dutch, and the hotel staff is Indonesian.

Holland America Line acquired a 50 percent interest in Windstar in 1987 and purchased the remainder of the line in 1988. In 1989, the Windstar headquarters moved from Miami, FL to Holland America's Seattle, WA, base. Subsequently, Holland America Line/Westours and its Windstar division were purchased by Carnival Cruise Lines.

Windstar provides a cruise unlike any other. It's very unstructured, emphasis is on the sea, on watersports, on casual explorations of less-frequented ports. There are none of the large-scale activities inherent in most cruises. Decor in muted leathers, polished metals, hand-finished woods, skylight spaces - give the vessels the ambiance of a private yacht, upscale yet casual. The ships' shallow drafts enable them to anchor at secluded coves and less frequented ports, giving them itineraries inaccessible to larger vessels.

There's an excellent array of watersports equipment water-skis, wind surfers, inflatable boats and a small gym and saltwater swimming pool. The ships also have libraries and casinos. Dinner is served in the dining room in single, open sittings, with a loose dress code specifying only "casually elegant." Breakfast and lunch are served al fresco or in the upper deck Veranda, which converts to a disco at night. Cabins, all identical, are outside and among the best designed at sea. They have ample storage, sleek bathrooms, refrigerators, TV/VCRs. Windstar passengers are generally professional or executive couples in their 30s, 40s, and 50s, well-traveled, but not necessarily experienced cruisers. Many guests are quite active, participating in the watersports and port visits, while others, relieved to be away from the stress of their busy lifestyles, are content to totally relax and do absolutely nothing.

Wind Star follows these same Windward and Leeward island itineraries from January to April, returning in October; $1,995 to $2,695. The *Wind Star* sails the Mediterranean, out of Nice, in summer and fall; $3 ,195. Fares quoted are for seven-day cruises; there are also some longer voyages. Tipping is not required, but tips are accepted (most customers gladly tip for extraordinary service).

WORLD EXPLORER CRUISES

Montgomery St., Suite 1001
San Francisco, CA 94111

Ships: SS Universe.
Destination: Alaska.
Description: Extensive shore excursions. On-board lecturers. Two-week cultural and educational cruises of Alaska aboard the SS UNIVERSE. Nearly 100 hours in eight ports of call. Glacier Bay and Yakutat Bay/Hubbard Glacier cruising. Itinerary includes Glacier Bay, Yakutat Bay/Hubbard Glacier, Juneau, Skagway, Sitka, Ketchikan, Valdez, Wrangell, Seward, Victoria, B.C. and the Inside Passage.

Cruise Agency Directory

As a courtesy for the tremendous amount of time and energy spent by our research editors, we have placed their three respective agencies listed alphabetically.

Eppie Epstein - Cruiseland, USA
19562 Ventura Blvd
Suite 200
Tarzana, CA 91356
(800)-767-7447

Bob Falcone - Cruises, Inc.
Pioneer Business Park
5000 Campuswood Drive
E. Syracuse, NY 13057
(800)-854-0500

Nancy Kelly -Kelly Cruises, Inc
Oak Brook Executive Plaza
1315 W 22nd Street
Oak Brook, IL 60521
(800)-837-7447

Of course, these are not the only agencies that sell cruises. For a complete listing of CLIA and/or NACOA affiliates, please write:

Cruise Lines International Association (CLIA)
500 Fifth Avenue, Suite 1407
New York, New York 10110

National Assoc. of Cruise Only Agencies (NACOA)
3191 Coral Way, Suite 630
Miami, Florida 33145

Glossary of Booking Terms

ACCOMMODATION—(See Room)

ADD ON—A supplementary charge added to the cruise fare, usually applied to correlated air fare and/or post cruise land tours.

AFT—Near, toward or in the rear (stern) of the ship.

AIR/SEA—A package consisting of the two forms of travel, i . e ., air to and from the port of embarkation as well as the cruise itself.

BAGGAGE ALLOWANCE—That amount of baggage, generally consisting of the passenger's personal effects, carried by the cruise line free of charge.

BASIS TWO—The cabin *rateperperson* applicable to a cabin capable of accommodating at least two persons . Also referred to as double occupancy.

BOOKING—A telephone request to a line's reservtions department to secure an option on a cabin.

CABIN—(See Room)

CATEGORY—A price gradient of similar cabins from the most expensive to the least expensive, or vice versa.

CLASS—Extinct on most cruises . On some trans-ocean voyages denotes an overall level of ambience and cost, such as "First Class", "Tourist Class" or "Transatlantic Class." Cruises are generally termed: one-class service.

CONDUCTOR'S TICKET—A free cruise ticket usually associated with groups of passengers traveling together, the entitlement to which is governed by each Line's policy.

CRUISE FARE—The actual cost of the cruise excluding all extras such as taxes, port charges, airfare, gratituties and the like.

DEBARKATION—Exiting from the ship.

DECK CHAIR—Open deck chaise lounge which is generally provided on a complimentary basis.

DECK PLAN—An overhead diagram illustrating cabin and public room locations in relation to each other.

DEPOSIT—A part payment of the cruise fare required at the time of booking to secure the cabin being reserved.

EMBARKATION—Entering or boarding the ship.

FORWARD—Toward the fore or bow (front) of the ship.

FINAL PAYMENT—Payment of the full cruise fare plus any necessary or agreed extras, such as taxes, air add on, preparatory to issuance of correlated travel documents.

FIRST SITTING—The earlier of two meal times in the ship's dining room.

FLY/CRUISE—(See Air/Sea)

GRATUITIES—The passenger's personal expression of thanks (tips) to the ship's service personnel for services received.

GRT—Gross registered tonnage, i .e ., a measurement of 100 cubic feet of enclosed revenue earning space within a ship. (See Space Ratio)

GUARANTEE—The cruise line' s promise that the passenger will sail on a stated voyage in a specified price catagory or type of cabin, at an agreed rate no higher than would ordinarily apply for that voyage, which may result in an improvement of accommodations at no additional cost.

GUARANTEE SHARE FARE—Acceptance by some lines of a single booking at the cost-saving double occupancy rate, with the understanding that the client is willing to share use of the cabin with a stranger of the same sex.

INSIDE—A cabin having no windows or portholes to offer a view of the sea, or of the river.

LOWER BED—A single bed placed at the conventional height from the floor. MIDSHIPS—In or toward the middle of the ship; the longitudinal center portion of the ship.

OFFER—The cruise line ' s commitment for accommodations then available which may be suitable to the passenger' s needs or wishes.

OPEN SITTING—Free access to unoccupied tables in the ship's dining room, as opposed to specific table assignments.

OPTION—The cruise line ' s offering of a specific cabin (or guarantee) for a specified period of time during which the passenger decides whether or not to accept. Acceptance is confirmed either by a deposit or final payment.

OUTSIDE—A cabin having window(s) or porthole(s) offering a view of the sea, or of the river.

PASSAGE CONTRACT—Detailed terms of responsibility and accountability found in the cruise ticket.

PETS—Any ordinary domesticated bird of animal. None are carried aboard cruise voyages.

PORT—The left side of the ship when facing forward.

PORT CHARGES—An assessment which also includes port taxes, collected by the line and paid to a local government authority.

PORTHOLES—Circular "windows" in the side of the ship's hull or superstructure.

PORT TAXES—A charge levied by local government authority to be paid by the passenger. In some air/sea packages port taxes are included in the final price.

QUAD RATE—An economical per person rate available to individuals for quadruple occupancy on a guarantee share basis.

REVIEW DATES—A periodic evaluation of the progress of the sale and promotion of a group combined with attendant cabin utilization.

ROOM—The passenger's room, stateroom or personal accommodation.

SAILING TIME—The actual hour at which the ship is scheduled to clear the dock and sail.

SECOND SITTING—The later of two meal times in the ship's dining room.

SHARE BASIS—(See Guarantee Share Fare)

SHORE EXCURSIONS—Off-the-ship tours at ports of call for which an extra charge is usually applied.

SINGLE OCCUPANCY—Sole occupancy of a cabin which is designed to accommodate two or more passengers in which instance a premium is ordinarily charged.

SPACE RATIO—A measurement of cubic space per passenger. Gross Registered Tonnage divided by number of passengers (double occupancy) equals Space Ratio. (rounded to nearest whole number)

STARBOARD—The right side of the ship facing forward.

STATEROOM—(See Room)

STOPOVER—Leaving the ship at a port of call and rejoining it at a subsequent port of call or upon the ship's return to the earlier port of call.

TENDER—A smaller vessel, sometimes the ship' s lifeboat, used to move passengers to and from the ship and shore when the ship is at anchor.

TBA—To be assigned.

TRANSFERS—Conveyances between the ship and other modes such as airports, hotels or departure points for shore excursions.

TRIPLE RATE—An economical per person rate available to individuals for triple occupancy on a guarantee share-fare basis.

TYPE—(See Category)

UPPER BED—A single size bed higher from the floor than usual (similar to a bunk bed) often recessed into the ceiling or wall by day.

WAITLIST—Not a guarantee, but the cruise line's endeavor to obtain accommodations for passengers on a first-come-first-served basis when all cabins are presently either sold, under deposit or under option.

Glossary of Nautical Terms

ABEAM—Off the side of the ship, at a right angle to length of the ship.

ACCOMMODATION LADDER—External folding stairway for access from ashore or from a tender along side.

AFT—Near, toward or in the rear (stern) of the ship.

ALLEYWAY—A passageway or corridor.

ALOFT—Above the superstructure; in, at or near the masthead.

AMIDSHIPS—In or toward the middle of the ship; the longitudinal center portion of the ship.

ASTERN—Abaft; or beyond the ship's stern.

ATHWARTSHIPS—Across the ship from side to side.

BACKWASH—Motion in the water caused by the propeller(s) moving in a reverse (astern) direction.

BAR—Sandbar, usually caused by tidal or current conditions near the shore.

BATTEN DOWN—To secure all open hatches or equipment for worthiness while under way.

BEAM—Width of the ship (amidships) between the widest point of its two sides.

BEARING—Compass direction, usually expressed in degrees, from the ship to a particular destination or objective.

BELLS—Audible sounding of ship ' s time—one bell for each progressive half hour to a total of eight, commencing at half past the hours of 4, 8, and 12.

BERTH—Dock, pier or quay (key).

BERTH—The bed or beds within the passengers' cabins.

BILGE—Lowermost spaces of the ship's innerstructure.

BINNACLE—The ship's compass.

BOW—Front or forward portion of the ship.

BRIDGE—Navigational and command control center of the ship.

BULKHEAD—Upright partition (wall) dividing the ship into cabins or compartments.

BULWARK—The side of the ship at or near the main deck.

CAPSTAN—Vertically mounted motor driven spindle used to wind in hawsers or cables.

CLEAT—Horizontal wedge-shaped device to which hawsers or cables are made fast.

COAMING—Raised partition around hatches or between doorways to prevent water from entering.

COLORS—A national flag or ensign flown from the mast or stern post.

COMPANIONWAY—Interior stairway.

CONNING—To superintend the steering of a ship.

COURSE—Direction in which the ship is headed, usually expressed in compass degrees.

CROW'S NEST—Partially enclosed platform at the top of the mast used by a lookout.

DAVIT—A device for raising and lowering the ship's lifeboats.

DEADLIGHT—A ventilated porthole cover through which light cannot be emitted.

DOCK—Berth, pier or quay (key).

DRAFT—Measurement in feet from waterline to lowest point of ship's keel.

DRAFT NUMBERS—Locaied at the bow and the stern to measure draft. Numerals are 6" high and 6" apart.

EVEN KEEL—The ship in a true vertical position with respect to its vertical axis.

FANTAIL—The rear or aft overhang of the ship.

FATHOM—1`~1easurement of distance equal to 6 feet.

FENDER—Anything serving as a cushion between the side of the ship and the dock or other craft.

FORE—The forward mast or the front (bow) of the ship.

FORWARD—Toward the fore or bow of the ship.

FREEBOARD—That outer part of the ship's hull between the waterline and the main deck.

FREE PORT—A port or place free of customs duty and most customs regulations.

FUNNEL—The smokestack or "chimney" of the ship.

GALLEY—The ship's kitchen.

GANGWAY—
Theopeningthroughtheship'sbulwarks(orthrutheship'sside
)andtherampbywhichpassengers embark and disembark.

GROSS REGISTERED TON—A measurement of 100 cubic feet of enclosed revenue earning space within a ship . (see Space Ratio)

HATCH—The covering over an opening in the ship's deck, usually of conisderable size leading to a hold.

HAWSE PIPE—Large pipe(s) in the bow of the ship thru which passes the anchor chain or hawser.

HAWSER—A rope of sufficient size and strength to tow or secure a ship.

HELM—Commonly the ship's steering wheel, but more correctly the entire steering apparatus consisting of the wheel, the rudder and their connecting cables or hydraulic systems.

HOLD—Interior space(s) below the main deck for stowage of cargo.

HOUSE FLAG—The flag which donotes the company to which the ship belongs.

HULL—The frame and body (shell) of the ship exclusive of masts, superstructure, or rigging.

INBOARD—Toward the centerline of the ship.

JACOB'S LADDER—A rope ladder usualy with wooden rungs.

KEEL—A longitudinal member extending from stem to stern at the bottom center of the ship from which all vertical framing rises.

KING POST—Vertical posts, usually in pairs, to which the ship's cargo cranes are attached.

KNOT—
Aunitofspeedequaltoonenauticalmileperhour(6080.2feet)asc omparedtoalandmileofS,280feet.

LATITUDE—Angular distance measured in degrees north or south of the equator. One degree approximates 60 nautical miles .

LEAGUE—A measure of distance approximating 3.45 nautical miles.

LEEWARD—(Pronounced - Lew-ard)—In the direction of that side of the ship opposite from which the wind blows .

LINE—Any rope smaller than a hawser.

LONGITUDE—Angular distance measured in degrees east or west of the prime meridian of Greenwich, England. Due to the earth's curvature, one degree of longitude will vary from approximately 60 nautical miles at the equator to zero at the north and south poles.

MANIFEST—A list or invoice of a ship's passengers, crew and cargo.

MIDSHIPS—(See Amidships)

MOOR—To secure a ship to a fixed place by hawsers, cables or anchor.

NAUTICAL MILE—6,080.2 feet, as compared to a land mile of 5,280 feet.

OUTBOARD—Away from the centerline of the ship, whether toward the ship's sides or beyond them.

PADDLEWHEEL—A wheel with boards around its circumference, and, commonly, the sole source of propulsion for riverboats.

PITCH—The alternate rise and fall of a ship's bow which may occur when underway.

PLIMSOLL MARK—One of a series of load lines marked on the side of a ship at the waterline to prevent overloading .

PORT—The left side of the ship when facing forward toward the bow.

PROW—The bow or the stem (the front) of the ship.

QUAY—(Pronounced - key) A dock, berth or pier.

REGISTRY—The country under whose laws the ship and its owners are obliged to comply, in addition to compliance with the laws of the countries at which the ship calls and/or embarks/disembarks passengers/cargo.

RIGGING—The ropes, chains, cables and the like which support the ship' s masts, spars, kingposts, cranes and the like .

ROLL—The alternate sway of a ship from side to side which may occur when underway.

RUDDER—That fin-like device astern and below the waterline which when tumed to port or starboard will cause the bow of the ship to respond with a similar turn.

RUNNING LIGHTS—Three lights (green on the starboard side, red on the portside and white at the top of the mast) required by international law to be lighted when the ship is in motion between sunset and sunrise.

SCREW—The ship's propeller.

SCUPPER—An opening in the bulwarks of a ship through which water accumulated on deck can flow freely overboard.

SOUNDING—Determining the depth of the water either by a weighted rope soundline in shallow waters or by electronic echo in deep waters.

SPACE RATIO—A measurement of cubic space per passenger. Gross Registered Tonnage divided by number of passengers (basis two) equals Space Ratio (rounded to nearest whole number).

STABILIZERS—A gyroscopically operated fin-like device extending from both sides of the ship below the waterline to provide a more stable motion.

STACK—The funnel or "chimney" from which the ship's gasses of combustion are freed to the atmosphere.

STAGE—the gangway of a paddlewheel steamboat.

STARBOARD—Right side of the ship when facing forward toward the bow.

STEERAGEWAY—A rate of foward or reverse motion necessary to allow the ship to "answer" a repositioning of the rudder (helm).

STEM—The extreme bow or prow of the ship.

STERN—The extreme rear of the ship, or toward the rear.

STOW—To fill or load a ship with cargo or provisions.

SUPERSTRUCTURE—The structural part of the ship above the maindeck.

TENDER—A smaller vessel, sometimes the ship's lifeboat, used to move passengers to and from the ship and shore when the ship is at anchor.

WAKE—The track of agitated water left behind a ship in motion.

WATERLINE—The line at the side of the ship's hull which corresponds with the surface of the water.

WEATHER SIDE—That side of the ship exposed to the wind or to the weather.

airfare SECRETS EXPOSED

Sharon Tyler & Matthew Wunder

Universal Information Corporation Publishing Co.

INTRODUCTION TO AIRFARE SECRETS EXPOSED

This book will save you a great deal of money on air travel. You will now have a resource guide which enables you to quickly understand and locate airfares that will save you hundreds, if not thousands, of dollars off the regular published prices. You will be traveling to exotic locations for a fraction of the cost of flying as a regular passenger. You will be flying on commercial airlines with others who will have paid 20% - 100% more for the seat next to yours.

You are about to join a small and exclusive group of people who have discovered the secret art of flying inexpensively. We believe you will never want to pay full price for an airline ticket again!

WHO READS AIRFARE SECRETS EXPOSED?

You would be surprised; we were. When this book was in the, "that would be a fun idea stage," we anticipated our readership to be fixed income people who otherwise were not able to travel -- students! Wrong! The profiles on the people who read obscure information to obtain the lowest airfare are often the same people who are in the financial position to not worry about how much they pay.

So why are people with the financial means to call up their travel agent and buy the first price quoted so enthusiastic about saving money on airfare? Answer: Obtaining the cheapest airfare is considered an art form and/or a thinking person's way of competing. We have spoken to hundreds of people who have either purchased our book or listened to our lecture. The common thread amongst all of our readership is a certain indescribable victorious feeling when they know the passenger sitting next to them paid three times the amount for the same seat.

TABLE OF CONTENTS

ORDER FORM

AIRFARE SECRETS EXPOSED

PLEASE SUPPORT YOUR LOCAL BOOKSTORE! We at UIC are committed to supporting local chain and independent bookstores. If you wish, you may write or fax your order directly to us.

POSTAL ORDERS: Sandcastle Publishing & Distribution Customer Service—Order Dept., P.O. Box 3070, South Pasadena, CA 91031-6070

PHONE/FAX MASTERCARD/VISA/AM. EXPRESS ORDERS:
Sandcastle Publishing & Distribution (800) 891-4204
Please fill out form and have your card # and expiration date available.

DISTRIBUTION TO THE BOOKTRADE:
Login Publishers Consortium (800) 626-4330
Competitive discount schedule, terms & conditions. Will work from official store purchase orders. STOP orders OK.

Please send the following books. I understand that I may return any books in unmarked and resalable condition for a full refund—for any reason, no questions asked within 7 days of receipt of the book.

Number of Books Ordered: ______ Cost of Books: $16.95 x ______ = ________
Sales Tax: = ________
Please add 8.25% sales tax for books shipped to a California address. ($1.40 for one book, $2.80 for two, etc.)
Packaging/Shipping: $3.75 for first book plus $1.25/add'l book = ________
TOTAL = ________

Please send my order to:

Name ______________________________
Address ______________________________
City ____________________ State ________ Zip Code ________
Daytime Phone Number with area code first ____________________